THE PURSUIT OF THE REAL

British figurative painting from Sickert to Bacon

The Pursuit of the Real

British figurative painting from Sickert to Bacon

Edited by Tim Wilcox

with essays by Andrew Causey, Lynda Checketts and Michael Peppiatt

Published by Lund Humphries
in association with Manchester City Art Galleries

Copyright © 1990 Manchester City Art Galleries
and Lund Humphries

First edition 1990
Published by
Lund Humphries Publishers Ltd
16 Pembridge Road London W11
in association with
Manchester City Art Galleries

British Library Cataloguing in Publication Data
The pursuit of the real : British figurative painting from
Sickert to Bacon
1. British paintings, history
I. Wilcox, Tim   II. Manchester City Art Gallery
759.2

ISBNO 85331 571 X

This is the catalogue of the exhibition
THE PURSUIT OF THE REAL :
BRITISH FIGURATIVE PAINTING FROM SICKERT TO BACON

Exhibition organised by Manchester City Art Galleries

Registrar : David McNeff
Photographic Research : Honor Giles
Publicity : Imogen Lock
Foreman Furbisher : Roy O'Neill

Exhibition tour :

10 March–22 April 1990
Manchester City Art Gallery
Mosley Street, Manchester

10 May–8 July 1990
The Barbican Art Gallery
The Barbican Centre, London

28 July–16 September 1990
Glasgow City Art Gallery
Kelvingrove, Glasgow

Designed by Alan Bartram
Made and printed in Great Britain by
BAS Printers Ltd, Over Wallop, Stockbridge, Hampshire

Exhibition sponsored by Manchester Airport plc

Contents

Foreword and acknowledgements

In recent years there has been a growing awareness of the strengths of British figurative painting and there have been several exhibitions devoted to individual artists included here. However, this is the first exhibition to show important contemporary painters alongside those who developed modern ways of painting from observation in the earlier years of this century: artists such as Walter Sickert, David Bomberg and William Coldstream. The exhibition argues the connections between them across a range of different styles and we are particularly pleased to be able to mount it here at Manchester City Art Gallery where we have taken the opportunity to include works from our own important collections.

An exhibition of this nature invariably involves a great deal of planning and discussion over a long period of time and relies heavily on the exceptional generosity of both artists and lenders as well as the committed efforts of colleagues on the Gallery staff. This is no exception and there are many individuals to whom I must extend my thanks for their various and invaluable contributions.

First of all I would like to thank the artists who have given their support to the exhibition and offered advice on the selection of their pictures. Particular thanks must also go to Manchester Airport plc for kindly agreeing to act as major sponsors for the exhibition and the Paul Mellon Centre for Studies in British Art for a grant towards the cost of production of the catalogue. This has enabled us to reproduce the substantial part of the exhibition in colour, while sponsorship has enabled us to bring important works over from the Continent. I would also like to thank the Museums and Galleries Commission without whose help and advice this exhibition would not have been possible.

Andrew Causey, Lynda Checketts and Michael Peppiatt have contributed informative and illuminating essays which in their respective ways offer contexts for the work of the artists in the exhibition within the broader development of British and European figurative painting. Such perspectives are particularly important when such a small number of painters is singled out for appraisal and I would like to thank them for making such an important contribution.

I would also like to thank all of the members of the Gallery staff who put large amounts of time and effort into the exhibition and I would like to express my particular appreciation of the achievements of Tim Wilcox who not only organised the selection of the exhibition with characteristic energy but who also edited and contributed significantly to the catalogue.

I am particularly pleased that the exhibition can be seen in both London and Glasgow as well as in Manchester and this has been made possible by the efforts of Jane Alison and John Hoole at the Barbican Art Gallery, London and Julian Spalding and Deborah Haase at Glasgow City Art Gallery.

I am indebted most of all though to the large number of individuals and institutions who have either generously agreed to part with their pictures for the duration of the tour, or who have assisted in tracing pictures and securing loans and I would like to extend my thanks to Judy Adam, Lorcan O'Neill and Robin Vousden of the Anthony d'Offay Gallery; William Joll of Thomas Agnew & Sons; Jill Constantine and Isobel Johnstone at the Arts Council Collection; Dr Wendy Baron; Margaret Bennett; The Ben Uri Society; Birmingham City Museums and Art Gallery; The British Council; The Syndics of the Fitzwilliam Museum, Cambridge; Girton College, Cambridge; Richard Cork; William Darby and the Browse and Darby Gallery; Dundee Art Gallery; The Scottish National Gallery of Modern Art, Edinburgh; The Royal Albert Memorial Museum and Art Gallery, Exeter; Lord Faringdon; Jeffrey Solomons and Fischer Fine Art Ltd; The Forward Trust Group; Glasgow City Art Gallery and Museum; Nigel Greenwood; Roberts & Hiscox Ltd; Henry Meyric Hughes; The Ferens Art Gallery, Kingston-upon-Hull; Bernard Jacobson; Leeds City Art Galleries; Mr and Mrs Donald Lenox; The Calouste Gulbenkian Foundation, Lisbon; The Trustees of the National Museums and Galleries on Merseyside (Walker Art Gallery, Liverpool); The University of Liverpool Art Collections; The Museum of London; The Thyssen-Bornemisza Collection, Lugano, Switzerland; Valerie Beston and Geoffrey Parton of Marlborough Fine Art (London) Ltd; Torquil and Anne Norman; Oldham Art Gallery; Andrea Rose; The Royal College of Art; Dr Peter Rumley; Mr Carl von Schmieder; Sheffield City Art Galleries; Sir Stephen Spender; Robert Stoppenbach and the Stoppenbach and Delestre Gallery; The Trustees of the Tate Gallery and Richard Morphet; Lord Walston; Colin St John Wilson and last, but by no means least, all those kind and generous individuals who have lent anonymously.

RICHARD GRAY
Director
Manchester City Art Galleries

Editor's Preface

Since the mid-1970s there has been a growing public awareness that a strong and varied group of artists have steadily been working away at developing a traditional, figurative based painting throughout the heyday of the avant-garde. The first important pointer towards a serious reassessment of the strengths of this traditionally based painting was R. B. Kitaj's *Human Clay* exhibition at the Hayward Gallery in 1976 and a number of important exhibitions have taken place since then which have given the artists associated with what Kitaj dubbed the 'School of London' their proper recognition.

The 1980 exhibition at the Royal Academy proclaimed 'A New Spirit in Painting' and mixed committed figurative painters of long standing with artists whose work had more recently shifted towards figurative imagery. However, what lies behind this exhibition might be described as an 'Old Spirit in Painting' and it attempts to show some of the connections between our most important figurative painters, working today with all the confidence and power of maturity, and those artists who advanced realist painting before the Second World War: Sickert, Bomberg, Spencer and Coldstream.

What they have in common is a shared belief in the weight of the tradition of European art as a positive virtue, not as something to be shaken off by superseding movements, but a touchstone against which to measure themselves. Secondly, they are engaged in the intensive study of the visually perceived world, rather than symbolic orders, and, thirdly, they make paintings about the experience of modern life. The pursuit of the real is the dynamo which drives these artists, while the knowledge is constant that the results will always become something different in the making. This exhibition provides a rich interplay of connections while showing the quality of achievement of those British artists who have looked upon the world, often against the grain of artistic and intellectual fashion, to give us paintings which will endure.

There are a number of individuals who have given me support and assistance throughout the formation of this exhibition. First of all I would like to thank Lynda Checketts who offered advice, guidance and encouragement at every stage and who has made an invaluable contribution to the catalogue. I would also like to thank the artists who have taken time to discuss ideas about their own work and have offered important insights into the concepts behind the exhibition. In particular I would like to thank John Lessore, Leon Kossoff and John Wonnacott. I have also discussed many ideas with the other two contributors to this catalogue, Andrew Causey and Michael Peppiatt, and I would like to thank them too. Finally I must echo the sentiments of the Director and extend my thanks to all those kind and generous individuals and institutions who have contributed in their various ways.

TIM WILCOX

Tim *Wilcox*

The Pursuit of the Real

A moment of complete happiness never occurs in the creation of a work of art. The promise of it is felt in the act of creation but disappears towards the completion of the work. For it is then that the painter realises that it is only a picture he is painting … Were it not for this, the perfect painting might be painted, on the completion of which the painter could retire.
Lucian Freud [1]

Freud's remarks on the nature of painting the reality of the world might be applied to any of those artists who have sought, or are seeking, the means to make significant paintings about the visible world in our century. There is an expressed anxiety about the disparity between intention and result. The task of the committed realist painter in the pursuit of the expression of emotions about the three-dimensional world remains one of acute challenge where the only tools are a refractory mix of pigment on a flat surface and the optical sensations of the eye. To follow this course is something which requires a strong discipline so as to avoid giving in to the easier satisfaction of balancing and harmonising the picture surface without further recourse to the subject. Each individual picture becomes almost a by-product of the process; left in a state of definitive incompletion and something which is common to nearly all these artists is a slow and painstaking method carried out over periods of time seemingly at odds with the pace of life elsewhere. Pictures begun years before will be returned to and reworked with a ruthless erasure of forms which no longer seem true to the picture's conception.

An acute awareness of time, human frailty and mortality is shared by these painters rather than a concern with timeless certainties, ideals or a programmatic, prescriptive kind of art. The foundation of this kind of painting is in the humanist culture of the Renaissance where artists from Giotto onwards discovered the expressive potential of the human form, and a belief in the common heritage of this figurative tradition is a firm and passionate conviction held by them all.

Sickert, whose writings are extraordinarily rich in their range and depth, wrote at the height of the early years of modernism about a genealogy of art stretching back into history (see Lynda Checketts' essay below for an analysis of the rôle of education in preserving this). [2]

This notion is repeated by Frank Auerbach who adds Bomberg and Sickert to the chain and concludes: 'it is not simply technical; spirit and attitude come into it'. [3] It is this shared sense of 'spirit and attitude' that brings the artists who are shown here together with their immediate mentors. The sense of an incomplete project played out over a long historical timespan which can be engaged with to create new statements about the modern world without being a progression on the work of the past, merely different, makes these artists modern but not 'modernist'. Modernism's historicist programme of development sought to bring art into a culturally significant relationship with the advancements of science and the programmatic and developmental thrust of social change. However, these noble intentions led to a debasement whereby changes of style were sought and encouraged with increasing pace and radicalism was taught as an end in itself. The result has been a loss of foundation of any sort – something which cannot be said of those artists shown here who have worked at odds with these developments but not without intelligent awareness of them.

The term which might still best describe these painters is 'realists'. They are concerned with the fascination of visual experience and with painting recognisable people and things. They are not concerned with finding equivalents for a higher reality behind or above the world of things – a metaphysical reality beyond the world of experience. Realism as an artistic term takes us back to the nineteenth century and covers both the work of the Impressionists and of less artistically radical painters concerned with the perceived facts of the world. Closely related to it was the positivist philosophy of Auguste Comte and John Stuart Mill who believed all knowledge of human experience to be an empirical science predicated on what was verifiable through observation. [4] These ideas formed a significant part of the intellectual environment of the realist painters who sought a similar solution by being impartially concerned with the precise description of visual facts and not with why things are as they are. Observation became more artistically important than convention and the boundaries between the ugly, the beautiful, even the horrific were all to be collapsed into the arrested moment with the impartiality of the scientist.

Degas in his almost anthropological investigations of dancers and women ironing or bathing, with his ability to make compositions from what were, on the face of it, the most unlikely and unidealised groupings of figures and settings, exemplified this intention. However, he differed crucially from some of his contemporaries in holding firm to the importance of past artistic conventions. An understanding of form which followed from within the tradition should always be applied to the search for the surprise and unexpected truth and beauty which could be found in hitherto extra-artistic subject-matter. This was the crucial lesson that he taught Sickert and which enabled Sickert to break away from Whistler's aestheticism. This and the importance of working from drawings.

As we move through the world our everyday visual experience is usually less than consciously thought out. We recognise certain places, people and things which carry us through our lives and to which we attach particular emotions without often analysing why we do so. The painter concerned with making images of this must be trained into seeing as a mode of conscious thought and must understand how to describe objects in space through the use of perspective, anatomy, scale, distance, space, light, an understanding of movement and so on. The primary tool for doing this is drawing exercised at speed and honed through constant practice. Sickert learned how drawing could be used to seize and hold a memory of a particular scene, incident or moment in such a way as to lock into it all the information necessary for working it into a painting away from the event. Sickert's acuity of observation enabled him to dispense with any form or detail extraneous to the suggestion of a particular mood or, in his two-figure compositions of the Camden Town period before the First World War such as *Hubby and Marie c.* 1912 (**3**), a sense of psychological tension. In order to remain true to the original conception contained in the drawing Sickert would square it up for transferral to the canvas. His distrust of working in front of nature was the result of a fear that a procession of images and sensations, no matter how small, would detract from the vividness of the compressed moment and this he would strive to maintain in the painting leaving brushmarks free and loose where they were outside the focal point of his gaze.

Sickert's colour, often derided as sludge-like in the Camden Town period or excessively brash in his later years, is in fact among the most inventive and refined in twentieth-century painting. A restricted palette of ochres, umber, burnt sienna, indian red, viridian green, he would invigorate with an azure blue or a Venetian pink or orange the colour of drapery in a Veronese which would suddenly, and with marvellous economy, harmonise the whole picture as it does in the portrait of *Victor Lecour* 1922-4 (**6**) for instance. A concern with crusty, impastoed pigment in his Camden Town period and in later years extremely dry paint thinly knocked out onto increasingly coarse canvases showed how much Sickert was interested in the modernist concern with facture but never at the expense of his traditional concerns with the figure.

In Sickert's extraordinary *Portrait of Hugh Walpole* of 1929 (**7**) he found a way of treating photographs – usually snapshots and newspaper photographs (not 'artistic' photographs) – which could find in them information he had previously acquired through drawing but without becoming enslaved to the rendering of the photograph's surface facts. The more raw, untechnical and detached the photograph the better. He had written in 1924 that 'the consequences of the invention of photography are throwing their weight in the scale against what was called "realism"',[5] and in 1929 that 'a photograph is the most precious document obtainable by a sculptor, a painter, or a draughtsman ... To forbid the artist the use of available documents, of which the photograph is the most valuable, is to deny to a historian the study of contemporary shorthand reports'.[6] These views contrasted with the one he had held some thirty years earlier that, 'In proportion as a painter or a draughtsman works from photographs, so is he sapping his powers of observation and of expression. It is

much as if a swimmer practised in a cork jacket, or a pianist by turning a barrel organ. For drawing, which should express these dimensions, is substituted a kind of mapping'.[7] What Sickert meant and indeed maintained in later years, was that the photograph was a seductive and enfeebling shortcut to the unskilled but a source of revelation and inspiration to the artist experienced in looking and drawing. This was to have particular implications later for the way artists like Bacon, Andrews and Wonnacott have used photographs in contrast with the deadening reproduction of surface engaged by American Super Realism of the early 1970s.

Andrew Forge, writing eloquently of Sickert's *Portrait of Hugh Walpole* discusses the way in which the loose, apparently arbitrary and hastily scrubbed brushstrokes over the blue underpainting are made coherent by the precise positioning of what few key details there are: the point of the chin, the nose, ear and spectacle frame 'each driven into place in the constellation like a rivet'. He calls it an 'old man's painting in an old language ... He does not step outside it or question it'.[8]

However, Sickert did question his pictorial language and he drove it to the limit of its possibilities as he engaged with other forms of popular mechanical reproduction in the late 1920s and 1930s as if to test painting's strength against them. Very much a part of this process was Sickert's use of Victorian engravings and popular prints which he called 'English Echoes' and Richard Morphet has pointed out how these late works testify to 'a pre-occupation ... with the mystery of time, the enigmatic relationship between "then" and "now"'.[9] This is particularly evident in what Helen Lessore cites as Sickert's last work, *The Temple Bar c.* 1941 (**10**).[10] Taken from an old engraving made before Christopher Wren's massive gateway had been removed from its original site in 1878 (and re-erected in Theobald's Park), the painting brings together many of Sickert's ideas about the craft of painting and reality. Composed from a restricted palette of creams and golden brown suggesting sunset through fog or mist, offset by a few dabs of indian red, it has the austerity and weight which led Helen Lessore to compare it with late Titian – an impression enhanced by the massive presence of the architecture. The squaring-up (often done by studio assistants in Sickert's late years – emphasising his belief in painting as a craft) is not simply left showing through, like a 'shirt hanging out', as Coldstream put it talking of his own construction marks,[11] but is *re-emphasised* at the surface of the picture as if the process had come full circle. As the spectator tries to make spatial sense of the image and what it depicts the grid cuts across it with its independent logic governed by the scale of the drawing/engraving in relation to the scale of the canvas. It acts as if we were looking at the picture through a barrier preventing access and pulling us always back to the fact of the surface itself. This tension between surface and the marks that make us 'see-in' spaces and things, what Richard Wollheim calls, 'twofoldness'[12] is made a virtue by other painters in this exhibition but rarely with such vividness. The ambiguity about space, time and authenticity is compounded by the origin of its subject in the engraving. Is the reality in the engraving itself, the memories of a past age which Sickert lived through himself, the fact of the architecture originally recorded (and perhaps offset by the

David Bomberg *Ronda: In the Gorge of the Tajo* 1935

picturesque placing of the cabs in relation to it), in the paint itself
or as a painted image? In the end its strange, even tragic, grandeur
is achieved in what it has become and not through what it references.
Sickert's engagement with realism in his late years was never less than
a process of deeply serious critical enquiry, aware that the world is
not just something which exists simply but is always and inevitably
altered in our attempts to describe it.

Of the artists who made the most use of Sickert's example between
1920 and the mid-1950s when a younger generation began to make
its presence felt, the key painters are David Bomberg and William
Coldstream with Stanley Spencer, temporarily setting aside his mys-
tical vision of secular harmony, to produce his own idiosyncratic
contribution in a remarkable series of nudes and portraits.

Bomberg had attained some measure of early artistic success and
notoriety with his youthful and precocious Vorticist paintings of the
early war years and the period immediately preceding the war. Like
many other modernists, when he experienced the full horror of the
front it led to a crisis of faith in modernism's anti-humanistic aspects
(particularly those of Futurism and Vorticism). In any case the artistic
coteries, with the exception of Bloomsbury, had been decimated by

1919. After a period of transition he felt the need to re-establish the
basis of his art, spurred in part by financial necessity. While others,
led by Picasso's example (taken up by Bloomsbury), moved towards
a nostalgic classicism which nervously attempted to reassert permanence and stability in the face of a modern world which had been
shattered, Bomberg began to draw upon his early training to find a
way of looking at the world again. As a child he had learnt by copying
Holbein and then in 1905 had been taught the importance of drawing
by Sickert's friend and associate, Walter Bayes who was a great
admirer of Degas. This foundation was reinforced by Sickert himself,
whose life drawing classes Bomberg attended at the Westminster
Technical School. This training had been put in reserve by an energetic and enthusiastic young man responsive to the arrival of modernism in England in the shape of Roger Fry's exhibition, *Manet and the
Post-Impressionists* in November 1910 and in its rapid changes and
development over the next few years in which he became a key figure
in spite of the fact that he was still a student at the Slade School and
had yet to achieve a mature style.

In his Jerusalem pictures begun in April 1923 Bomberg worked his
way through what he had learned earlier from Fred Brown and Henry
Tonks at the Slade about the importance of drawing with an awareness of structure, and the laws of optics and perspective. Painting both
in the intense, razor-sharp, light of the day where colour was
bleached out but structural lines were intensified and shadows
deepened, and by the low-level intensity of moonlight, he found for
himself a way of working directly from the subject. Through the
topographical precision of paintings like *Jerusalem, Looking to Mount Scopus*
1925 (**12**) Bomberg reassessed what he had first admired in Cézanne's
late work, not in the light of Fry's and Bell's formalism, but as an
example of an exacting visual enquiry into space and mass. One can
see in this painting Bomberg's precisely laid brushmarks following
vertical, horizontal or diagonally recessive lines in an attempt to emu-
late Cézanne's painterly correspondence to planar disposition.

The beginnings of a way to re-inject his emotions into his painting
after this period of necessary submission to a rigorous discipline of
observation were to be found in the sparing and atmospherically evo-
cative small landscapes such as *Mount Zion with the Church of the Dormition:
Moonlight* 1923 (**11**) and first became fully realised on his trip to
Toledo in 1929. In *Toledo and River Tajo* 1929 (**13**) he applied a new
vigour and rhythm to a more highly keyed palette (despite his written
assertion that the cliff-top city was dark and sombre) with brushstrokes slashing and sweeping into the steep gorge from the precarious huddle of dwarfed buildings above.

Behind this change of style lay two further strong intellectual influences on Bomberg's work: Bishop Berkeley's *Essay Towards a New Theory
of Vision* (1709) and John Fothergill, editor of the *Slade Magazine*, who
took up Berkeley's ideas and developed them in relation to the teaching of drawing. Berkeley proposed that there is no direct correlation
between the sense data of vision and objects we know through touch.
Visual appearances give 'signs' to the understanding of objects experienced by touch but are not co-extensive with them even though we
effortlessly make the connection between an object seen and its tan-

gible presence because it is natural to us. Forthergill, in his entry on 'Drawing' for the 1910-11 edition of the *Encyclopaedia Britannica* expounded his own extension of these ideas of tactile experience:

> … all drawing of forms that merely reproduces the image on the retina, and leaves unconsulted the ideas of touch, is incomplete and primitive, because it does not express a conception of form which is the result of an association of the two senses.[13]

Bomberg, in *Toledo and River Tajo* and in the majestic works he produced on subsequent visits to Spain in the 1930s, worked his way towards expressing his own understanding of this union of the visual and the tactile in a way which had not been achieved before. The most successful paintings are those which seem to court an almost physical danger; paintings like *Ronda: In the Gorge of the Tajo* 1935 (**14**) where Bomberg positions himself at the bottom of the vertiginously steep gorge as if the possibility of climbing out of it to a redemption beyond presents the possibility of falling, just as the problem of making the experience real through painting presents the possibility of failure on the canvas. The brushstrokes applied with swiftness and force have an anxious physical energy and their colliding and mingling creates a vision of a terrain convulsed by some seismic force. In the best of his later landscapes, like *Castle Ruins, St Hilarion, Cyprus* 1948 (**18**), a lighter, feathery (though no less vigorously painted) touch in brilliant pinks, ochres and oranges creates an ecstatic, celebratory atmosphere of blazing light. Bomberg had raised landscape painting to a new level in twentieth-century art whereby he found a way of using it as a vehicle for feelings about life and mortality as well as space, light and mass.

Bomberg's responses to the softened atmospheric effects and gentler formations of the English landscape were always more muted, and it is interesting that his most successful work painted in Britain is *Evening in the City of London* 1944 (**17**) where the motif is like those of many of his Ronda and Cyprus landscapes: St Paul's rising solid and serene, its dome pointing to the top of the canvas as if to a life beyond, while Bomberg's angle of vision falls away below him into an abyss of scorched and ruined buildings like desolate canyons.

Stanley Spencer, who had been a contemporary of Bomberg at the Slade, represents an interesting and idiosyncratic development of realist painting in twentieth-century British art. He had never seriously become a part of the avant-garde but had developed out of the study of the Quattrocento an autobiographical and religious vision applied to the secular but with a grounding in observation. Objective recording of the visible world was, however, paramount in the landscapes he sometimes referred to as 'pot-boilers' but which are anything but, even though they were made to assist his income. In a landscape like *Cottages at Burghclere* c.1930-1 (**20**) Spencer discovers surprising compositional juxtapositions by accurately describing, and not altering for the sake of conventional harmony, an already picturesque scene. It is abundant in details such as roof tiles and individual leaves but without losing this Pre-Raphaelite element to the underlying perspective and the accurate rendition of the fall of light. It is, in its way, a kind of a realism dictated by a rural romanticism in its evoca-

tion of a secret and harmonious place which stands in contrast, not only to the urban and prosaic view of the Euston Road School or Camden Town, but also to the stark and tormented nudes and portraits he was to paint in the mid-1930s after the break-up of his first marriage to Hilda Carline and then of his second to Patricia Preece.

In *Self-Portrait with Patricia Preece* of 1936 (**21**) and in the other nudes he painted in 1935 and 1937 the figures are painted so close-to that they only just fit into the picture frame giving an impression of uncomfortable proximity to the spectator. This is compounded by Spencer's utterly matter-of-fact plotting of folds, sags and blemishes in a type of nude painting which was wholly new in the context of British art and might be more properly thought of as naked portraiture[14] – something which Lucian Freud was to develop independently with even greater intensity in more recent times. The picture disturbs still more though because by including himself seen from behind as a spectator within the picture (in a device like that used by Caspar David Friedrich to create empathy with his landscapes of solitude and melancholy), Spencer attempts to heighten the sense of sexual tension and to narrow his own distance as the spectator-painter.

However, although Spencer's gaze is supposed to appear as if it were meeting Patricia Preece's she is shown staring wistfully out and beyond in rejection of his presence and judging from the angle of Spencer's head it is impossible that he can be looking at her, but rather to one side and into the distance. Both are lost in their separate reveries despite the apparent intimacy. Only through the formal means of the picture can Spencer hope to recover the suggestion of any physical union. His neck and shoulder share the same line as the curve of her right thigh and his nose is only a fraction from joining with the sweeping line of her breast, but both we and Spencer know that even through their represented selves he cannot bridge the physical and psychological divide.

Spencer's evocation of sexual desire and frustrated fulfilment was particularly shocking to a public used to impossibly idealised marble-skinned nudes bearing no relationship to the particulars of an individual and they met with anger and derision from artists like Alfred Munnings[15] whose own work was typical of the debased, picturesque brand of modern genre painting which dominated popular taste.

Where Spencer only departed from his own painting cycles of a personalised, secular religion in these extraordinarily frank nudes and certain correspondingly tense portraits such as *Hilda, Unity and Dolls* 1937 (**22**), Coldstream attempted to make a realist method serve social aims. First of all by consciously adopting a democratic art corresponding with 'the popular idea of what things look like', as Coldstream put it writing about Holbein.[16] He began this project with Graham Bell in 1936-7 prompted by the economic privations of the slump but although their images were to do with people and ordinary places in the Camden Town manner they did not display the kind of overtly illustrational socialist themes prevalent in the Artists' International Association whose artists tended to suffer from an assumption that a correct ideological position could compensate for painterly incompetences. Coldstream was additionally spurred in this direction by his friends W.H. Auden, Christopher Isherwood and Stephen Spender whose portraits he painted and who were attempting to do something similar in their use of an accessible, even colloquial style of poetry applied to intently serious themes.

Early contact with Cézanne while a student at the Slade, and with Sickert's teaching on drawing, helped Coldstream to break away from the conflicting attraction of a self-consciously advanced art under the then dominant intellectual influence of Fry and Bell. The same influences which had helped to reformulate Bomberg's style with an emphasis on finding in Cézanne not the beginning of abstraction but a commitment to a methodically objective realism were also crucial to Coldstream. In a climate of conflicting artistic choices he needed them to convince him that realism could still be achieved without abandoning intellectual content. With his portraits of 1937-8 such as the magnificent *Stephen Spender* 1937 (**27**) he reinvigorated the art of portraiture by abandoning the deliberate ennobling of the features and demonstrative, emphatic brushstrokes in favour of tightly regimented vertical strokes made with the sable brush in thin paint in a manner akin to the effect produced by Degas which Bacon has called 'shuttered form'.

Coldstream's desire to exclude his subjective responses to both his subject and his painting led him on from these small, scanning brush-strokes to a more complex system of horizontal and vertical marks forming a notational web around and across the subject. He would take these measurements with the thumbnail against a brush-handle held by his outstretched arm; each small mark being colour-coded and then compared and adjusted with each previous mark. Lawrence Gowing has described this method as being

like a shuttle passing to and fro to weave the ultimately credible fabric, [it] begins to leave at each passage a mark like a vivid stitch of the very thread that draws the form together.[17]

Coldstream's attempted detachment and his austere method and col-our have led to descriptions of his 'sobriety', 'sense of duty' and 'Northern and Protestant' temperament, yet for all his stated empiricism he has testified to the same anxiety about the ultimate possibility of realism as Freud:

Certainly one designs, modifies, modulates, simplifies, selects, and exaggerates, since painting is not a scientific record of fact but a record of fact enlarged and modified by one's reaction to it, and the most realistic painting can be nothing like reality.[18]

The realisation of this kept him fascinated with discovering anew an extremely limited range of subject-matter: nudes from the time of his Slade professorship in 1949 when models from the life room became available for sittings, private and commissioned portraits and prosaic city-scapes (see **32**). The extreme self-effacement and austerity of Coldstream's work, coupled with indifference from all but a small band of enthusiasts, has ultimately prevented it from reaching that popular audience he had so much hoped for as public taste has become governed by the kaleidoscope of sensation offered by the new visual landscape opened up by the media.

Figurative painting with a realist outlook has had a chequered

William Coldstream *Portrait of Stephen Spender* 1937 (detail)

history of development since the Second World War in a period in which not only did art schools greatly expand but avant-garde art was officially sanctioned and taught. As prosperity returned in the mid-1950s it brought with it a cornucopia of images through television, advertising, colour supplements and packaging. The brief period of 'kitchen sink' realism in the early 1950s (discussed in more detail in Andrew Causey's essay below) which had produced very uneven results was effectively killed off by the eruption of American-style consumer democracy. Consequently those artists who were continuing to develop the lessons for an artistically challenging figurative painting demonstrated by Sickert, Bomberg and Coldstream, did so in an atmosphere of almost monkish seclusion, retreating into their studios or finding their own personal corners of London's streets which seem to have an air of secrecy and privacy while they are yet public places.

The key painters are those who have come to be grouped together as 'The School of London' (see Michael Peppiatt's essay below): Andrews, Auerbach, Bacon, Freud and Kossoff. R. B. Kitaj is usually included too but his work points in a somewhat different direction involving, as it does, a strong emphasis on literary, symbolic and philosophical material which puts his painting at a remove from the concern with direct visual engagement. However, as stated earlier, the purpose of this exhibition is to attempt to move to one side of this definition of a school and to concentrate on the core of painters who do not subsequently add additional content to the 'gross material fact' of visual reality.

Although Bacon is exclusively associated with post-war British art he is in fact of the same generation as Coldstream. His work has provided a touchstone for figurative artists since his *Three Studies for Figures at the Base of a Crucifixion* was first exhibited in 1945, despite the fact that his art and methods are highly inscrutable and hermetic and have not provided a practice which could be emulated and adapted in the way that Coldstream's could. He has gone further than Bomberg had in completely re-inventing the terms on which realism could be predicated without disrupting essential connections with the art of the past. On the way he has absorbed, one might say devoured, Surrealism on the one hand and the saturated colour of 1960s abstraction on the other in a way which has completely transcended any sense of those influences.

In one of his many revealing interviews with the critic David Sylvester, Bacon has stated his approach to the problem of realism:

I believe that realism has to be re-invented. It has to be continuously re-invented. In one of his letters Van Gogh speaks of the need to make changes in reality, which become lies that are truer than the literal truth. This is the only possible way the painter can bring back the intensity of the reality he is trying to capture. I believe that reality in art is something profoundly artificial and that it has to be re-created. Otherwise it will be just an illustration of something which will be very second-hand.[19]

Bacon sets this in relation to the ever increasing determination of the visual world by the camera and the cinema. In order to avoid the possibility of the 'illustrational' and the 'second-hand' arising in the presence of the subject he has abandoned even Sickert's approach of working from quickly made drawings. Instead he has taught himself to combine the process of discovery that is drawing directly with the act of painting itself.

His engagement with photographs, whether those of Eadweard Muybridge, photo-booth portraits of himself, snapshots of friends as used for the *Portrait of Henrietta Moraes* 1965 (**45**) or medical photos, has been a constant process of questioning the supposed 'truth' which photographs assume. Our mental idea about other people is not just composed of their appearances but of our emotions and sensations accumulated over a period of time and these can often be triggered by a photograph. Although Bacon has had sitters he finds their presence distracting and disquieting:

… if I both know them and have photographs of them, I find it easier to work than actually having their presence in the room. I think that, if I have the presence of the image there, I am not able to drift so freely as I am through the photographic image[20]

I don't want to practise before them the injury that I do to them in my work.[21]

The features by which we conventionally recognise another person: the eye, mouth, the profile of the nose and hairline would appear, on first evidence, to contain the likeness of the sitter in Bacon's work, and yet they turn out to be more stylised elements than the twisting swathes of paint which combine physical facts with characteristic movements. What he is trying to capture beyond the elements conventionally connected with likeness is the sitter's interiority – a sensation of what it might feel like to be *inside* his subjects. He conceives of himself and others not in terms of 'character' or 'personality' but as 'nervous systems' which control the muscle actions and movements which make an individual's posture and body-language distinct. These, Bacon suggests, are more vivid in recollection.

Michael Andrews also makes use of photographs as reference material but he has also drawn directly from the subject. Both life drawings and photographs were employed in the creation of the magnificent early work, *The Family in the Garden* 1960-2 (**33**) which Andrews painted in the garden of his parents' house in Norwich. The fairly thin paint and measured restraint show a clear homage to Coldstream who had been a crucial influence during Andrews' time at the Slade. The ordered harmony of the composition with his family aligned along a graceful curve connects material fact with a record of a particular social order. This was in complete contrast with the paintings of nightlife which immediately followed. In *The Colony Room I* 1962 (**34**) Andrews placed the figures casually with an eye to the uncomfortable, unaesthetic groupings that are captured in party snapshots – the ones where people end up with bright red eyes in compromising positions. While the figures on the left of the picture are relatively free within the spaces they occupy, the central group of Henrietta Moraes, Bruce Bernard and Lucian Freud are uncomfortably and tightly compressed. This picture stands at the beginning of a series of paintings Andrews completed during the 1960s which deal with the psychological interactions of people in large gatherings: often as in *The Deer Park* 1962 and *All Night Long*, 1963-4, they deal with occasions which require a certain formality and socially controlled behaviour to begin with, but which end in an excess with the falling away of social masks.

Andrews has been fascinated by how the isolated individual behaves in relation to others and his series of balloon pictures of the early 1970s such as *Lights II: The Ship Engulfed* 1972 (**35**) resulted from seeing a photograph of a balloon in a newspaper while reading phrases from R.D. Laing and Alan Watts about 'the skin encapsulated ego' and 'the prevalent sensation of oneself as a separate ego enclosed in a bag of skin'.[22] The balloon-ego may be 'buoyant' or 'deflated', may ascend or descend accordingly, or, as in this painting, it may drift serenely through the shimmering enticements of the urban environment. Behind these pictures lay Andrews' fascination with Kierkegaard's writings on how an individual might make himself in relation to his surroundings and his perceived state of being, as well as engaging Andrews' own sense of the optimistic possibilities and community spirit which had prevailed in the 1960s.

If Andrews deals with social interaction or situations of psychological challenge Lucian Freud is almost exclusively concerned with the individual figure and paints directly from his subjects. Helen Lessore has described how he seems to have worked his way through the principal styles of the Renaissance in an almost programmatic attempt to find out for himself how painting from vision could be done, taking in the Northern technique of proceeding by small degrees across the form and then adding to this the Italianate grasp of the whole in as near to a single glance as possible. Indeed looking at Freud's paintings has the curious effect of giving one the sensation that one is looking at something which has always been there, even when the paint is barely dry. The breadth of understanding of the old masters is uncanny.

John Russell's description of Freud's 'particular kind of steadfast scrutiny [which] involves a long, slow stalking of the thing seen'[23] is apt in respect of all his work but particularly the small painstaking portraits of the early 1950s such as *Girl with Beret* 1951 (**49**). The sitters seem to have a barely contained agitation as if the huge, alert eyes had been caught and fixed in the process of searching out the nearest cover like a startled animal in a car's headlights. Again, in the portrait of John Minton the lips appear to quiver and the neck muscles are tensed as if he were drawing short, shallow and nervous breaths. There is in these works a tightly controlled, crystalline finish and an obsession with minutiae which he was to break away from in the early 1960s to find ways of making the paint itself more varied and of stressing its material quality as well as its illusionistic function. By the late 1960s his new range and confidence led to the large and mysterious *Large Interior, Paddington* 1968-9 (**50**) in which the possibilities of the figure in relation to its setting were explored. Here the juxtaposition of the small child, with which Freud takes daring liberties of form which nevertheless convince, and the indoor linden tree which looms and writhes, shows Freud's awareness of the possibilities of his technique. The leaves are painted with a precise awareness of their states of growth and with the enamelled precision of his early studies of organic forms, while the child's body is more freely and loosely brushed to suggest the agility and potentiality of young muscles.

This awareness of the nature of living things – their various patterns and stages of growth – has become even more acute in recent years. The particular forms of an individual are now more interrogated than questioned. The intense and fearful illumination of a 500-watt bulb serves to sharpen and intensify them. There is no escaping into shadow permitted and the relentless probing picks up every nuance, every vein, mole, blotch, tuck and fold of skin. The desire seems to be to chart an organic presence in its cellular particulars in the hope that through these its individual presence will be brought onto the canvas. In his explorations he has found a way of understanding how an individual's features have come to be shaped and aligned as they are, for instance in the extraordinary portrait of *Frank Auerbach* 1975-6 (**51**) in which the forehead looms forward like some kind of strange boulder, crushing and bending the nose and cheeks under its weight.

In the 1980s Freud's work has become grander and more complex in conception and he has developed his ability to portray several figures in one setting without giving way to the narrative element he, like Bacon, abhors. A fact which also explains his common practice of treating his sitters as anonymous. In the magnificent *Two Irishmen in W.11* 1984-5 (**53**) Freud is acutely attuned to the differences in age and posture of the two men and has found just the right con-

sistency and type of brushstroke to correspond to either the material of their clothes, the bones of a hand or the overcast drabness of the roof-tops seen beyond through the studio window.

Like Bacon, Freud has found a way to invest realism with a new purpose, but only by closing his world to the prospect of irrelevant intrusion – artistic or otherwise:

My work is purely autobiographical. It is about myself and my surroundings. It is an attempt at a record. I work from the people that interest me, and that I care about and think about, in rooms that I live in and know. I use the people to invent my pictures with, and I can work more freely when they are there.[24]

Leon Kossoff and Frank Auerbach have tended to suffer from being constantly referred to as if they were siamese twins. They both studied at St Martin's School of Art and at the Borough Polytechnic with David Bomberg and began by using an extraordinarily heavy impasto of earth colours which gave their portraits and studies of building sites a sombre, tragic mood. However, they have developed and diverged substantially since then and their paintings have become distinctively their own.

Auerbach is perhaps the artist here who is most consistently concerned with the scope for surprise and discovery to be found within small variations of the same basic method applied to a severely restricted subject-matter. The basis of this process is dedicated exploration through drawing, what Auerbach calls 'mental grasp'. He produces hundreds of drawings in stages on the same sheet, constantly eradicating and reworking the image with a succession of instinctive strategies for exploring the forms before him without resorting to a descriptive, illustrational process, and resisting the temptation to experiment with marks for their own sake. No stage contains less effort or desire to experience the whole subject but if it does not seem to hold some life of its own which is also true to the subject in some way then it will be ruthlessly abandoned. His paintings follow the same path, large brushstrokes acting like sweeps of the charcoal and boldy following their own trajectories. As they surge across the forms certain effects of colour and mark fall off from them like vapour trails as wet paint is driven across wet.

In the early *Head of E.O.W.* 1954 (**38**) the colour is predominantly yellow ochre, ivory white and a dense black, only offset by the most sparing use of a deep crimson and a sea-green balancing each other top left and bottom right. Paint has been accumulated into a dense layer as a result of successive exploratory stages being piled on top of each other so that the whole image has the effect of a bas-relief. An effect which is unintentional as the head is tonally constructed and not sculpturally modelled. It is an extraordinarily compressed painting, the head bowing down under its own weight in the narrow confines. This concentration of the image and the way in which the face is described by a series of circular brushstrokes moving across the forehead, round the side of the face and under the chin to create a halo-like effect led Stephen Spender (who once owned the painting) to describe it as having 'the look of a scared object, like the image in a shrine encountered at a crossroads'.[25]

In the 1960s and 1970s Auerbach found his way out of any residual associations with sculpture which might arise by scraping off all preceding stages which did not satisfy him and starting again from only the faintest trace of the original image. This refinement of his working method brought his work into a meaningful tension between the destructive and creative urges in a particularly modern way. The paintings also became notably contemporary through Auerbach's use of brilliant primary and secondary colours in complete contrast to the works of the 1950s and in accordance with the general spirit of the times which favoured bold colour use. But there was another precedent for this change to be found in the way that Sickert had advanced his painting from the dark, encrusted Camden Town works towards the bright and breezy colour inventions of the 'English Echoes'.

Sickert's influence on Auerbach has been a formative one and certain direct parallels might be made between, for instance E.O.W. on Her Blue Eiderdown 1965 (**39**) with its matter-of-fact pose, the way in which the limbs are arranged and described with quick directional marks, and its organisation about a single focal colour, and Sickert's Le Lit de Cuivre c.1906 (**2**) which is similarly bold and intense.

In more recent years the sense of experiment has become increasingly adventurous and the paintings less directly like their subjects. Faced with Head of Catherine Lampert II 1988 (**43**) we cannot immediately be sure of what each mark is doing. While we can register the brushmarks forming the nose or an eye socket, others, like those clustered about the neck, seem to probe the skeletal structure but without describing it in any familiar way. The image has been arrested at this moment rather than any other because Auerbach has instinctively recognised the configuration, with its mixture of purpose and accident, as corresponding to some grain of longed-for truth about the subject. This fleeting correspondence in the storm of the creative process which Kossoff has called 'glimmering towards light' gives the painting its own life and presence, what the artist calls 'a new species of living thing'. As with Freud, Auerbach's concern with particular and subtle states is part of an almost obsessional desire to 'play a trick with time' and arrest or cheat the inevitable path towards death, to 'move an experience a few years ahead or a few years back, or turn the curious nullity of a silent man by himself in the studio into something that happens, with tremendous luck, 300 years later to somebody who is visiting a gallery'.[26]

Kossoff places the same primary emphasis on drawing as an independent and artistically essential activity, but he brings to his work a broader range of subject-matter and a concern with the life of particular places. In the early works like Father Seated in Armchair 1960 (**56**) the massive accretion of paint is used to create the sense of an individual cowed by an enormous load, what John Berger called 'the crushing weight of suffering',[27] yet at the same time the massive forms of the limbs are tough and resilient as a steel hawser.

As happened with Auerbach's painting, Kossoff's colour lifted during the 1960s but never became so high-keyed, remaining more restricted and subtle. In many of the very beautiful landscapes of the 1960s like Railway Landscape near King's Cross, Summer 1967 (**57**) Kossoff recorded the effects of a particular time and season on the landscape

in a manner more like that of the Impressionists than of the Expressionists with whom he is frequently, but somewhat erroneously, associated. What the writhing, energetic paint describes is a site typically 'unaugust' and 'unsmartened' in the Sickertian sense. Indeed Kossoff seems to seek out forgotten corners which have their own quirky resilience and trace of human use in contrast with the office blocks which threaten to engulf these pockets of resistance like a vast invading army massing on the horizon.

Among Kossoff's finest paintings are some of the works he has painted of the booking hall and entrance to Kilburn Underground station from 1976 onwards such as Outside Kilburn Underground, Spring 1976 (**58**). In this work the figures are simultaneously locked into the space of the painting and into the web at the surface. The painting has been made from repeated drawings done until 'the pressure of the accumulation of memories'[28] is forced into being. The scurrying figures, both enfolded and imprisoned by the overarching railway bridges, have been imprinted on his memory so firmly that 'the painting, like a flame, flares up in spite of oneself';[29] in spite of the hold of the remembered image. The palette is dominated by various shades and densities of grey but Kossoff has enlivened the whole picture with the most sparing use of kingfisher blue, viridian green and wine red with a sensibility for the effects of simple harmonies. Divided almost centrally between the two principal figures, the one leaving, the other entering the booking hall, each stooping, self-absorbed and closed to the world about them, the painting arrests a moment in the daily flux. The site, of course, is not a station on some romantic route to adventure in another place but a part of the routine coming and going of London life ruled by the clock. It is utterly prosaic in its function and place and yet through Kossoff's painting it is made into a monumental image of resilience in the face of human frailty. In this sense it is reminiscent of Auden's great poem, 'As I Walked Out One Evening' about time and the need for love which supports us in the inexorable march towards death; which begins

> As I walked out one evening
> Walking down Bristol Street
> The crowds upon the pavement
> Were fields of harvest wheat[30]

Kossoff's figures have a bending, quavering quality as they are pulled this way and that by the forces of life, like Auden's stalks of wheat, and yet within their individual existence is a small part of the monumental, coursing presence of humanity, its 'deep river', which is Kossoff's concern as much as it was Auden's.

John Lessore has quietly been making his own monumentality out of what he has called 'the mystery of everyday life'.[31] Having grown up surrounded by Sickerts it is perhaps hardly surprising that he sets great store by Sickert's use of drawings to capture a subject with maximum economy and speed. Lessore's paintings are quiet and contained with a deceptive ease which disguises the concentration of their making. He is concerned, primarily, with the problem of making powerful and convincing compositions out of his subject-matter of people engaged in various forms of activity, whether a frenetic communal dance as in La Farine, Villemoustaussou 1981-4 (**63**), or a moment of intimacy and absorption in family life in paintings like *Paule and Rémi I* 1963 (**61**). While the aesthetic means of making a taut and convincing design are foremost in his thinking, his observation is such that he can tellingly depict subtle nuances of posture and bodily expression.

The Garth 1982-3 (**64**) is one of Lessore's most accomplished and intriguing paintings. It shows students at Norwich School of Art entering the rear of the main building from which the picture has been painted. Dominating the composition, the building known as the Garth is seen across a grassy area which contains the ruins of the old monastery and the original cloister-garth. It is architecture which has a softened time-worn look which Lessore had found so stimulating growing up in war-ravaged London. The inventiveness of the composition and the way the figures are disposed testify to Lessore's interest in capturing surprising groupings of people seized from the continuity of physical and optical movement by his drawings. While the central space is airy and expansive the foreground consists of the geometric configurations created by a wooden ramp which form a kind of architectural border to the picture. Bounding the picture on the left is a solitary, stooping figure, perhaps collecting a bicycle, while on the right, crowding in under the shadow of the main building, is a group of self-absorbed students which is tightly compressed into the corner of the composition implying movement beyond the picture frame. The painting is formed from brushstrokes which are creamy, elastic and cursive, moving quickly across the forms which have already been held and made accurate by the drawing, while the colour is used sparingly but inventively to contribute to the suggestion of a subtle mood. Lessore shows the clear influence of Sickert in the way he restricts himself to a very limited palette dominated by muted pinky browns, flesh tones, ochres and ivory, with just a very sparing use of strong Venetian colour on the students' jackets which enriches the picture and prevents it from becoming sombre. It is a painting of remarkable poise and simplicity which creates a mysterious mood of quietly contained conviction in the pursuit of knowledge.

While Andrews took Coldstream's influence and moved off on his own idiosyncratic explorations, Euan Uglow and John Wonnacott have pursued the example of Coldstream's 'straight painting' more closely. In many respects their work is similar, while in others it diverges significantly. Both are challenged by the use of monocular vision and are fascinated with the rational order of geometry. They both render their subject-matter in a very clear light which gives emphasis to the boundaries of forms.

Euan Uglow does this with the most severely restricted subject-matter and means. His staple is the traditional studio nude but set in relation to an artificial space contrived by the artist himself with geometrical markings and the odd prop used as if by a minimalist stage designer. What concerns him is the vastly complex challenge presented by the model, especially in some of the more athletic poses he gets them to adopt, and the backgrounds he uses provide both structural reference points and create contrasts and tensions with the human form. To these governing factors is added the artificiality of the picture plane itself which has its own geometry and integrity governed by the size and format of the canvas (usually designed by Uglow according to a system of classical proportions), the centre of vision chosen and the distance from the model. In the case of the last two factors in *Nude, from Twelve Regular Vertical Positions from the Eye* 1967 (**67**) the viewpoints chosen were multiple and the position of the eye so close to the model that only fractions of the body could be recorded from each viewpoint, resulting in a strangely elongated figure which nevertheless seems believable just as the inventive distortions of Ingres' nudes seem correct.

As Uglow gathers information about the model it is plotted by a measuring system adopted from Coldstream and is locked together with the precision of a master carpenter constructing a cabinet. There is the simultaneous fascination with the surface design created, the shape of each plane and their interlocking relationships providing that clarity and beauty possessed by certain cystalline structures. The resultant shapes are often surprising and inventive but their integrity to what is seen keeps the decorative impulse duly subordinated.

In the early nude, *The German Girl* 1961-2 (**66**) the figure fills the picture with an austere monumentality which removes attention from the background, which is cursory and muted, although hints of its future rôle in the design are present, but not yet utilised. This was to come with increasing confidence in unifying his drawing and the confident discovery of the boundaries of planes. These have, after all, to be fabricated as we do not see limbs with the jade-warrior effect which Uglow's paintings produce close to. Since the late 1960s the figures are often set against large slabs of unmodulated colour which serve to highlight the contained figure by the contrast of their flat, bold simplicity with the minute complexity of form and subtlety of coloration and paint modulation in the description of the body in paintings like *Curled Nude on a Stool* 1982-3 (**69**).

John Wonnacott sets himself the problem of organising extremely ambitious figure groups in huge light-filled spaces. These test to the utmost his belief in the possibility of a rational understanding of the exterior world and the ability to describe this through a trained and structured order of seeing. His insistence on monocular vision and the rendition of both local colour and tonality under various conditions of light using a fairly flat, even paint surface, has led to superficial and inaccurate comparisons with the photo-realists. In fact his use of the camera to reinforce the memory behind the drawings he continuously makes in front of the subject, and on which his painting is securely grounded, has more in common with the seventeenth-century artist's use of the camera obscura. It provides him merely with focused details from the transient events which concern him and other, traditional, mechanical aids such as the perspective frame, are more significant tools. However, nothing is more important to him than the goal of achieving likeness through hand and eye alone.

He recalls that initially he had been attracted by Expressionist painting while at the Slade and had responded only warily to the instruction in observation up until his post-graduate year in 1963. It was then that he began to realise that 'it was through a direct confrontation with appearances that painting would yield to me its deeper excitements, but a need to relate the formal mechanics of the picture directly to my knowledge of the way the eye "sees" made me develop a slower, detached approach'.[32]

In part this realisation was spurred by seeing Michael Andrews' *The Family in the Garden* 1960-2 (**33**) when it was shown at the Beaux Arts Gallery in 1963 and Wonnacott embarked on his own treatment of this theme which carried his work through the 1960s and into the early 1970s. His work, which concentrated on the life of his family and records of his father and grandfather (who were both dying), was accompanied by a number of peculiarly intense self-portraits such as the *Grey Self-Portrait* 1967-74 (**72**) in which the residual desire for emotional effect is checked and contained in the way Wonnacott gives equal emphasis to the complexity of space and the effect of the intense vertical light source, which becomes itself 'a dominant object in the design'. During this period Wonnacott experimented with angles of vision of 100° or more using strict perspective geometry. Anamorphic distortions at the edges of the picture surface correspond to the curvature of the retina and to the areas of indistinct reception at its edges where there are few of the cones which give us the clear information about things at the centre of the gaze. He was able to create paintings which could be fixed to one specific viewpoint in all its particulars as if the image were a single moment of vision. These discoveries were brought to bear with magisterial force in the commission from British Caledonian to paint a portrait of its director, Sir Adam Thomson. In these portraits of 1985-6 (**74**, **75**) Wonnacott's latent romanticism is held perfectly in balance with the rigour of a rationally organised construction. In the daytime portrait (**74**) Thomson's head is painted with a scrutiny that allows its concentrated shape to dominate the maze of detail accumulated towards the centre of the picture. The position of his portrait close to the centre of vision (the exact centre of the picture) and closer still to the position of the main vanishing point (just to the right of the centre) makes the connection between the mode of the organising structure of the picture and that of the director as controller of the intense and purposeful industry behind and below him in this modern secular cathedral. Every inch of the painting is carefully considered in terms of its function and relation to the whole just as the hangar itself is demarcated with the precise functional efficiency of the engineers who have created it.

The relation between light, space, time and memory has become increasingly the subject of his recent pictures of the mud flats near his home in Leigh-on-Sea such as *The Crabbing Bridge* 1986-7 (**76**). Here the vast bowl of blazing light, painful to the eyes as it glares off the vistas of clouds and the wet mud and tide pools, is anchored formally only by the horizon line exactly bisecting the centre of the picture. This painting has the quality of a memory recovered from childhood where all is impossibly joyous and serene, yet it is specifically about a time and place in the present as much as were the paintings of the Impressionists. The movement of light across the sky and through the day, with all its infinite variations is the ancient marker of our numbered days and Wonnacott's painting seems to express this elemental quality as much as it is concerned with a contemporary vision of life.

Behind the realisation that the diurnal and nocturnal course will overtake us all in the end there is always the hope and desire of capturing and containing our experiences of life as they pass from time experienced to time remembered and this is the quest which gives these painters their special meaning and purpose.

Notes
1. Lucian Freud, 'Some thoughts on painting', *Encounter*, July 1954.
2. See also Lynda Morris (Checketts), 'The Excitement of Vision' in *John Wonnacott*, Marlborough Fine Art, London exhibition catalogue 1985.
3. Paul Bonaventura, 'Approaching Auerbach', *Metropolis*, 17 February 1986.
4. See Linda Nochlin, *Realism*, Harmondsworth 1971, p.23 and pp.40-3.
5. From Sickert's 'The Royal Academy', *The Southport Visitor*, Spring 1924. Quoted by Richard Morphet in *Late Sickert*, Arts Council of Great Britain exhibition catalogue 1981.
6. Sickert's letter to *The Times*, 15 August 1929. Quoted in *Walter Richard Sickert: Advice to Young Painters*, edited by Lynda Morris, Norwich School of Art Gallery exhibition catalogue 1986.
7. 'Is the Camera the Friend or Foe of Art?', *The Studio*, June 1893, pp.96-102. Sickert's comments were in response to this question which was put to a number of prominent artists of the day.
8. Andrew Forge, 'Sickert's portrait of Hugh Walpole', *The Listener*, 7 October 1965, pp.531-2.
9. Morphet, *op. cit.* n.5.
10. In a talk recorded in 1960 and broadcast in 1966. Cited in Morphet, *op. cit.* n.5, p.107.
11. Coldstream in conversation with David Sylvester, 'William Coldstream: "Painting given subjects"', *Burlington Magazine*, April 1977.
12. Richard Wollheim, *Painting as an Art*, London 1987, pp.46-7. Wollheim talks of a simultaneous experience of the image and the material marks which cause us to 'see-in' that image.
13. John Fothergill, 'Drawing', *Encyclopaedia Britannica*, London 1910-11. Quoted in Richard Cork, *David Bomberg*, New Haven and London 1987, p.25.
14. Spencer wrote that he wanted 'to be able to paint a nude from life and do it as I do a portrait. I mean not so quickly but taking my time'. Quoted in *Stanley Spencer*, Royal Academy of Arts exhibition catalogue, London 1980, p.141. Spencer did not like the idea of using professional models.
15. Munnings made a shabby attempt to have Spencer prosecuted.
16. 'The Art of Hans Holbein: a Revaluation', *The Listener*, 6 February 1947.
17. Lawrence Gowing, introduction to *William Coldstream*, Arts Council of Great Britain exhibition catalogue 1962.
18. William Coldstream, 'Painting' in *Art in England*, edited by R.S.Lambert, Harmondsworth 1938, pp.99-104. Reprinted from 'How I Paint', *The Listener*, 15 September 1937, pp.570-2.
19. Francis Bacon in *Interviews with Francis Bacon*, David Sylvester, 3rd ed. published as *The Brutality of Fact*, London 1987, p.172.
20. *Ibid.* p.38.
21. *Ibid.* p.41.
22. Phrases quoted in *Michael Andrews*, Arts Council of Great Britain exhibition catalogue 1981, p.65.
23. John Russell, introduction to *Lucian Freud*, Arts Council of Great Britain exhibition catalogue 1974, p.5.
24. *Ibid.* p.13.
25. Introduction to *Frank Auerbach: recent paintings and drawings*, Marlborough Gallery Inc, New York exhibition catalogue 1982.
26. Auerbach interviewed by Richard Cork, *Art & Design*, vol.4, no.9/10, 1988, p.21.
27. John Berger, 'The Weight', *New Statesman*, 19 September 1959, p.353.
28. Kossoff quoted in *Leon Kossoff*, Anthony d'Offay Gallery, London exhibition catalogue 1988.
29. *Ibid.*
30. W.H.Auden in *The English Auden*, edited by Edward Mendelson, London 1977, p.227. The poem was written in 1937.
31. John Lessore interviewed by Julian Spalding on 'Third Ear', Radio Three broadcast, 21 March 1988.
32. John Wonnacott, statement in *John Wonnacott: paintings and drawings*, Rochdale Art Gallery exhibition catalogue 1978.

Andrew Causey

The Possibilities of British Realism

The Pursuit of the Real starts with the leading Camden Town painter, Sickert, and traces the development of certain ideas about realism to the present day. But the concept of the real is not a stable one right through the century. The world today and the way we experience it has changed so much in eighty years that there is no simple definition of reality that will encompass the whole period. By concentrating mainly on figure painting, the exhibition has focused also on a particular aspect of visual reality.

'Each age has its landscape, its atmosphere, its cities, its people. Realism, loving life, loving its age, interprets its epoch by extracting from it the very essence of all it contains of great or weak, of beautiful or sordid, according to the individual temperament.' This Baudelairean declaration comes from the Camden Town painter Charles Ginner's manifesto 'Neo-Realism' published in *The New Age* in January 1914. 'Neo-Realism' was reprinted as the introduction to the catalogue of a joint exhibition of Ginner and Harold Gilman,[1] and it was endorsed – apart from a few quibbles – by Sickert.[2] In some sense it is therefore a manifesto of Camden Town painting in 1914.

The contemporary paintings of Ginner in which Neo-Realism is reflected include views of London with streets busy with people and traffic, while Gilman's paintings at the same time were portraits, domestic interiors and café scenes. These urban landscapes and genre studies reflect a desire to provide a truthful and objective picture of metropolitan life, from its new up-to-date motor buses to encounters in seedy rooming houses. It is a sturdy, serious kind of art that for the most part avoids the temptation to make the sordid picturesque or the modern glamorous.

In the intervening years the direct approach of Camden Town painting has given way to more complex visual languages. Ours is an age when experience of the outside world is conditioned by marketing techniques and the media: images are not only surrounded by unprecedentedly complicated patterns of meaning, but all of us who experience them are becoming increasingly well versed in their interpretation. The approach to reality implicit in Camden Town painting was relevant before the quickening of consumerism and media domination in the late 1950s, but has less impact today. Camden Town painting was realistic in the sense that it repudiated the picturesqueness of the Newlyn School and much other late Victorian painting and introduced a standard of unbiased objectivity. Its tenets remained serviceable so long as it was possible to believe that the objects in our immediate surroundings, directly presented, could be read with confidence in a single way. The rôle of marketing in consumer society has irrevocably changed our concept of reality. From Pop onwards the image-building strategies of the communications world, techniques of suggestion involving ambivalence and irony, have stimulated endless invention and oblique viewpoints in art.

In emphasising painters of the human figure, this exhibition focuses largely on work that is existential rather than social. Although it is concerned substantially with the work of living artists, many are painters associated with what has become known as the 'School of London', whose interests in general were established by the end of the 1950s, before the rôle of art in a consumerist world became problematic.

Sickert challenged accepted values which made any figure subject in a painting the representative of a social class: a peg, maybe, on which to hang fine clothes, or an object of pity if penniless and condemned to life on the breadline. Sickert asserted that a person was a breathing sentient being who ate, drank and loved, was flawed and vulnerable, but could also be worldly wise and endowed with the survivor's earthy wisdom. He brought to English art what his friend Degas and others had claimed for the French: the Bohemian's right of entry into the hitherto private world of the less privileged, access to a tough vitality that the increasingly conventionalised bourgeoisie lacked. 'No country', Sickert wrote, 'can have a great school of painting when the unfortunate artist is confined by a puritan standard to the choice between the noble site as displayed in the picture postcard, or the quite nice young person, in what Henry James called a wilderness of chintz'.[3]

Sickert's realism involved the portrayal of everyday life, but it was also a particular way of painting. He preferred thick *pâtes* (he used this French word) of paint in contrast to the thin *alla prima* application of his former master Whistler, or the swagger virtuosity of Edwardian drawing-room art – because he felt the substance of the paint was an affirmation of material reality. 'Sound drawing and painting proceeds by cumulations, by addition; decadence sets in when subtraction plays a large part.'[4] Figurative painters from Sickert to Bacon have been dubbed anti-modernist because of their disdain for abstraction. But surface texture, so important to many of the painters in this exhibition, is itself a preoccupation of modernism.

Sickert's view of the history of art was way ahead of his time. He instructed his students to look at social illustrators like John Leech and Charles Keene and satirists from Rowlandson to Cruikshank. An ironical, self-contradictory man, he refused to be pinned down to specific views, but had a perception of an alternative, socially critical strain in English art (draughtsmanship as much as painting), which was descended neither from the aristocratic tradition of eighteenth-

Stanley Spencer *The Resurrection, Cookham* 1924-6

century country house landscape and portraiture nor from Romanticism. The historical artists whom Sickert defended were often those who challenged accepted authority. But this does not infer that Sickert was himself either politically radical or a satirist. His approach is emotional and psychological. What he found stimulating about unmasking spurious claims and lampooning pomposity and posturing was the way this brought art back closer to human values and drew his audience nearer to real life. Sickert is important for many of the painters in this exhibition partly on account of his technique – his use of dense pigment and refusal to consider drawing as separate from painting – but essentially because he penetrated the defensive barriers people raise to prevent discovery by the world. He demonstrated that the flawed beings often excluded as subjects of art in fact displayed a complexity of human motivation and behaviour particularly worthy of study.

Camden Town brought ordinary people into British painting without stereotyping them: the Londoners of Sickert and Gilman never recall images on picture postcards, as Breton peasants and Cornish fishing people often do in the art of the Newlyn painters, nor can they be read as arguments for social reform as the underprivileged can in the art of late Victorian realists like Herkomer and Fildes. Sickert, it is true, had a strong sense of theatre, but he used it to accentuate human qualities such as pathos, dignity, and pride, and his designs never became rhetorical. Extending the subject-matter of art to give it a wider class basis was an achievement of Camden Town, but one that, even if two of the movement's leading artists, Gilman

and Spencer Gore, had not died early, would not necessarily have survived. The 1920s was a conservative decade and its art, like its politics, seemed concerned to show the old order resurgent, as if the pre-war political turmoil and the war itself had not changed things. There was little room for the Camden Town type of painting, and, in the main, figure painting altogether has an undistinguished history in England between the wars.

Stanley Spencer is an obvious exception and one who, especially when seen, as in this exhibition, largely through works of the 1930s, foreshadows in his own terms the problems faced by a later figure painter such as Bacon. There are many of Spencer's paintings that can be read in terms of Bacon's declared ambition to 'bring the figurative thing up onto the nervous system more violently and more poignantly'.[5] Since Spencer saw himself, and has been regarded since, as constructing a world of community and mutual benevolence, the comparison may seem odd. But Spencer's art has violent contrasts of mood, between the spiritual ease of the resurrected on the Last Day in the Burghclere designs or the *Resurrection, Cookham* 1924-6 and the torment in the 1930s of his nudes and Adoration series. He liked to think of himself as bringing people together, but even a painting of his own family, *Hilda, Unity and Dolls* 1937 (**22**) shows how figures can butt up against one another in terms of picture space but remain psychologically miles apart. The canvas is a patchwork of tensions in which not only mother and daughter but dolls as well play an active rôle. Though Spencer represented himself as painter of an optimistic world united in a vision of fraternity and love, a close study of his work suggests that this was an ungraspable panacea and that his life was fraught with growing anxiety as personal disasters in the 1930s widened the gap between vision and reality.

The series of nudes that Spencer suddenly painted in the mid-1930s of his second wife, Patricia Preece (**21**), certainly bears this out. Earlier British painters had not shown particular interest in the nude. Sickert broke the Victorian taboo against the naked female form – unless seen either as Venus or a fairy – with pictures that are frank and often voluptuous. They have casual poses that speak of a desire for naturalism, though knowledge of Sickert's ways suggests that the casualness is calculated and that pleasure in the nude body and even voyeurism are conscious elements. But there is always a dispassionate side to Sickert, who is cool, while Spencer, by contrast, examines fervently every detail of Patricia Preece's body. Sickert's nudes are rarely individualised, but Spencer's are identifiably of his wife, whose face is included. Unlike Sickert's Spencer's canvases are portraits as well as nudes.

Much of this exhibition is an expression in one way or another of loss of innocence, of the twentieth-century's discovery that the Enlightenment vision of harmony through education and beneficent institutions is flawed. From a modest beginning in Sickert's laconic jibes through Spencer's anguished frustration to Bacon's monumentalising of human animality is expressed a growing sense of disillusion and despair.

The history of figure painting in England in the first half of the century is sadly fragmentary. A painter like Mark Gertler, with a rigorous Slade education in drawing behind him and talent comparable with Spencer's, achieved much less than his early successes promised. British art has always been characterised by moments of collective energy and achievement, like the years 1910-14, and times of relative lethargy, such as the period after the First World War. In the past one reason for this was that artists did not have strong institutional support to carry them through periods of conservative taste and weak patronage like the 1920s. The Royal Academy has a particular responsibility here because of its traditional association with the humanist practice of figure painting, and a significant reflection on its rôle between the wars is provided by a group of resignations during the 1930s. Spencer left in 1935 in protest against the refusal to hang some of his own works in the summer exhibition. Sickert resigned the same year when the Academy refused support for the protest over the destruction of the Epstein statues in the Strand, and Augustus John surrendered his membership when his friend Lewis' portrait of T.S. Eliot was left out of the summer exhibition in 1938. In no case did the Academy act beyond its powers, nor were the three events immediately connected in any way. But the involvement here of no less than five of the most interesting practising figurative artists cannot be unconnected at a deeper level. In effect the Academy was being offered an opportunity to become the forum for exhibition and debate about the figure at a time when other artistic groups, the Surrealists and abstractionists, were finding their collective identities, but the offer was not taken up.

Spencer's combined energy and egocentricity gave him a degree of self-motivation that enabled him to survive. An example of a comparably talented painter who was less fortunate is William Roberts. Roberts' painting after the First World War developed in an individual way that combined the sharp geometrical forms of his own early Vorticism with a more pronounced figuration. He painted largely leisure themes, sports and popular entertainments, and also scenes of work. Roberts was very skilled at adapting Cubism to urban genre subjects. He had a strong sense of form which enabled him, despite the variety of narrative detail in his paintings, to create powerful and lucid designs.

The Times reviewer of his 1923 exhibition wrote: '*Dock Gates*, to name only one example, shows that Mr Roberts would be the ideal decorator of a municipal or commercial building, and it is indeed remarkable that the picture has not been secured by one of our shipping companies.' The same paper's critic later described Roberts as the nearest England had to a truly popular artist because he understood the richness of London life, and 'one feels that the man in the street would understand his pictures'.[6] It was sad that Roberts did not have the opportunity to design on a large scale that Spencer had at Burghclere and that he did not gain the support of Academy membership till the most exciting period of his art was past.

Spencer was fortunate in finding a private sponsor at Burghclere. Contemporary public commissions did exist: for the decoration of St Stephen's Hall, Westminster, and, from Brangwyn, for the House of Lords (rejected and now in Swansea Town Hall). But such patronage was mainly in the hands of conservative Academicians who were jealous of what they regarded as their own domain. Spencer's tremendous success at the first Academy summer exhibition where he showed, in 1934, aroused jealousy which undoubtedly contributed to his partial exclusion the following year. It was this kind of attitude that ensured that England had no Rivera. Spencer's painting was too personal, too intimately the product of his own private life and fantasies, to be called realist in a narrow sense, while Roberts' had by now acquired a poster-like simplification that gave it great presence and impact but was something different from the more detailed scenes of a Camden Town artist such as Gilman who had not undergone the influence of Cubism.

The dire economic condition of Britain in the 1930s with millions unemployed not surprisingly focused attention on the urban condition and led, in the short-lived Euston Road School, founded in 1937, to a redefinition of realism that owes something to Camden Town. Its leading member, William Coldstream has written: 'The slump had made me aware of social problems, and I became convinced that art ought to be directed to a wider public; whereas all ideas which I had learned to regard as *artistically* revolutionary ran in the opposite direction. It seemed to me important that the broken communications between the artist and the public should be built up again and that this most probably implied a movement towards realism.'[7] Coldstream had already briefly abandoned painting to work in documentary films, because he wanted to 'work in some medium which is by its nature more essentially of the present age, more easily accessible to a large number of people'.[8] Euston Road realism con-

William Roberts *Dock Gates* 1920

sisted of urban interiors and landscapes (a few of Bolton, because Coldstream and his colleague Graham Bell worked there for Mass Observation), and portraits.

While the Euston Road painters might have agreed with Sickert's contention that 'the more our art is serious, the more it will tend to avoid the drawing room and stick to the kitchen',[9] they would have dissented from his next sentence, which asserted : 'the plastic arts are gross arts, dealing joyously with gross material facts'.[9] Sickert's belief in painting as a process of addition and his generosity with his medium contrast with the dry, austere technique of Euston Road which was governed by the very puritanism for which Sickert expressed contempt.

Euston Road painting was grounded technically in the nineteenth century, in Degas, Whistler and Cézanne, and though Sickert was a

kind of honorary patron of the group, their work is not like his. Sickert's bohemianism and his gentle deflating humour signified his attachment, realism notwithstanding, to an aesthetic approach which Euston Road would have emphatically rejected. In so far as there is a link with Camden Town it is with the parsonic Gilman, a much straighter realist than Sickert with a commitment to Socialism. Even here, though, a distinction needs to be made. The unembroidered realism with which Gilman painted his landlady, Mrs Mounter, not only lacks the picturesque touches that Sickert sometimes added, but is also different from Euston Road portraits, which tend to be of the artists' friends and to be penetrating individual social studies. The portraits of Mrs Mounter are objective, and iconic in the sense that Gilman has made his subject stand for a type if not a class. The documentary realism of Coldstream's urban scenes can be understood

Harold Gilman *Mrs Mounter at the Breakfast Table* 1916-17

Graham Bell *The Cafe* 1937-38

William Coldstream *St Pancras Station* 1938

in terms of its challenge to existing ideas. In his depiction of St Pancras Station, which he got to know from visits to Bolton, he laid it out in a way that would be of use to a traveller. There is no romance of modernity in his representation of a locomotive, no picturesque incident to add human interest. Between the wars, when rail travel was expanding and heavily promoted by advertising, the most commonly experienced pictorial image of a train was on a poster, and the connection most frequently made there was between the train and the countryside. Railways were associated with historic monuments and places of special beauty, or, in the case of London Underground, with leafy suburbs composed of brick houses in seemingly endless summertime. For Coldstream, St Pancras is simply the other end of the line from Bolton. There is no implication that anybody is about to be transported to a sylvan paradise. Nor, on the other hand, does Coldstream construct an image of the blackened city as a foil to a sentimental vision of green fields.

The realist debate as initiated by Euston Road was not furthered by the war. This may at first seem surprising, as war industries and the Battle of Britain focused attention on factory work and city life, while the War Artists' Advisory Committee, which commissioned artists to record the home front as well as battle scenes, was concerned to promote art that would be popularly comprehensible. But the general effect of the war was to foster patriotic sentiment, and the approach of many artists tended towards the picturesque. Though Coldstream's paintings of ruined London retain his earlier objectivity, his influence was confined to a relatively small circle of artists. The war highlighted an important characteristic of English realism: popular taste prefers picturesqueness and the embellishment of objectivity with sentiment to realism in its more austere forms.

When the realist debate widened out again as the result of a number of exhibitions from 1952 and the polemical criticism of John Berger in the *New Statesman*, the influence of wartime picturesque romanticism was still being felt. Fifties realist art focused on Helen Lessore's Beaux Arts Gallery. The artists shown included John Bratby, Edward Middleditch, Derrick Greaves and Jack Smith, the core of the group who became known as the Kitchen Sink after an article of that title by David Sylvester in *Encounter* in December 1954.

Realism, Berger said, meant rejecting the generalising tendency of abstract art, obsessional esotericism (Bacon), and regressive psychological art (Moore), in favour of the ordinary and day-to-day. Berger argued that this would not lead to pedestrian painting if artists could succeed in sharpening the viewer's vision of common reality and thereby extend popular understanding of everyday subject-matter. He promoted this idea of a social realism as the basis of all his criticism, but acknowledged also the more radical concept of a properly socialist realism. The latter concept surfaced, for example, in a debate with Benedict Nicolson.[10] Berger asserted that art should be more than a medium of communication with the power to reflect on human actions: what mattered at that moment (1955) was the use of art as a weapon of the working class during the social crisis presented by the crumbling of the bourgeoisie.

Kitchen Sink painting did not simply mirror the views of its leading critical supporter. While it is possible to see how the miners and field workers of Josef Herman might fit into a socialist realist context (in fact Berger found Herman verged too much towards expressionism),[11] it is doubtful whether the Kitchen Sink painters themselves truly do. One of them, Jack Smith, specifically denied any intention in his painting beyond reflecting the environment in which he lived. Middleditch's scenes of Sheffield, on the other hand, gain their effect as much from theatricality as from realism. The inheritance of wartime Neo-Romanticism lasted a long time in England, not in a narrow stylistic way but in a tendency to treat painting as stage design. While there is nothing wrong with this in itself – an artist such as Edward Burra practised it brilliantly – it has little to do with objective observation as practised by Coldstream. In particular, Coldstream's objectivity resisted the idealising tendency of poster-type design which leads to flat synthesised images that are scenic in character. The art of Middleditch in the 1950s is flat and scenic, and in so far as it is realist at all, it has little to do with the Euston Road approach.

Bratby is a different kind of artist, attacking his subject more directly, without the picturesque qualities which characterise

John Bratby *Still-Life with Chip Fryer* 1954

Middleditch. That Bratby's art does not have the objectivity of Coldstream's, however, is more than just a matter of contrast between a lavish and flamboyant painter and an austere and puritanical one. Despite the suggestion of spontaneity that arises from Bratby's painterly virtuosity, this is not the case. Speaking of his 1954 paintings, Bratby has said: 'For models for my Table Top still lifes, I used the same table every time, and eating equipment from the kitchen of the house. The works are therefore absolutely contrived and artificially set up.'[12] A chip fryer is not plausibly seen hung on the back of a dining room chair and Bratby is not a naturalistic painter. His bold Post-Impressionist brushwork and high-keyed colour are reminiscent of the later Bloomsbury paintings of Bell and Grant, and his subjects can be read as revisions of Bloomsbury conversation pieces at a different social level. Though it can thus be argued that his art is class specific, the main preoccupation of the paintings is sensuous and emotional.

These designs are celebrations of common objects, their realism is an affectionate, haphazard embrace of the grocer's shelf.

In 1959 Berger regretfully admitted that social realism had failed, and the rapid evaporation of Bratby's considerable reputation, alongside those of the other realists, confirmed this. To understand the phenomenon it is useful to compare Bratby's uncritical endorsement of the common object in a stylistically regressive form with the near-contemporary art of Richard Hamilton. Hamilton's images of women in the home and of automobile styling inspired by American marketing programmes are both positive and critical. Hamilton's art is analytical rather than directly affirmative; it has something of the approach of the amused sociologist and, in contrast to Bratby's, it is stylistically advanced. Comparison between the artists was not made at the time because in the 1950s, when Bratby was acclaimed, Hamilton was ignored: by the 1960s the situation was reversed. This shift of opinion says a lot about the possible definiton of realism in modern painting. Different though Bratby's painting is from that of Camden Town, the same broad but direct embrace of the physical world encompasses both. That Bratby's painting in the mid-1950s looks old-fashioned today and Hamilton's modern is more than a matter of style: with Hamilton and later Pop artists and their successors, advertising, marketing and techniques of media presentation intervene in the perception of the world, an innocence of vision is jettisoned. The domesticity of Camden Town painting and of Bratby's lost its conviction because the traditional idea of home implied by a Bratby table top still-life carried less weight than it had. Growing concern with communication, and the forms and languages it adopts, meant that the one-to-one relationship of viewer to the object as a used and loved thing no longer seemed so interesting. Though not many years separate them in time, the tins, packets and bottles on Bratby's tables have nothing in common with Warhol's massed ranks of soup cans and Coca-Cola bottles. In a world in which marketing has come vitally to underpin production it is difficult to see that Bratby's vision can be recaptured.

Berger's position was founded on optimism, in the sense that ordinary people could influence the world they lived in. A realistic art could have a popular audience, he thought, and by sharpening perception of the world help people to embrace it. The failure of Bratby's painting to gain long-term acceptance suggests that people no longer saw their surroundings in the way Berger would have liked. When it came to figure painting, Sickert had recognised before 1914 that people were interesting not in so far as they were rational and responsible but because they were quirky and individual. Two world wars later, with the desperation of Spencer's 1930s canvases intervening, this irrationality was reflected, now without anything of Sickert's gentle humour, in the momentous despair of the canvases of Francis Bacon.

A review near the beginning of Berger's critical career of Bacon's 1952 exhibition at the Hanover Gallery illuminates the writer's position here: 'Everything then depends upon the content of the pictures [which included three 'Popes' and a zoo picture] and, since most of them are horrific, on the meaning of horror, disgust and loneliness

... I believe that Bacon's interpretation of such suffering and disintegration is too egocentric, that he describes horror with connivance – that his descriptions lack not only the huge perspective of compassion but even the smaller perspective of indignation.'[13] Bacon's horror, Berger concluded, was stimulating because it was remote, removed from the normal world. However, Berger's requirements for art were not part of Bacon's vision. Bacon's purpose was truth rather than compassion, and all his art expresses the conviction that the truth about the human condition can only be conveyed in terms of personal experience rather than as a social issue. Popes and apes are not a part of the everyday world. But Bacon believes that to show a man in the modern world through his everyday likeness is to condone the self-concealment, the raising of façades against the world, that people practise all the time. He feels himself forced into extremes in order to express truth. Pope and ape are metaphors for the highest and the lowest, but their aspects are merged, or rather the pope is caught in the involuntary gesture of a scream, an instinctual act characteristic of an animal.

Bacon's ambience of what he has called 'gilded squalor' is a baroque world of energy and excess which values brilliance and admits corruption. If Bacon is no longer able to show courtliness with the glamour of Titian or Velázquez, it is because he has called the bluff of accepted twentieth-century values – as Picasso did in the contorted late 1920s paintings of figures that Bacon has commended for wider study[14] – by tearing away the mask of rationality that is that world's self-protection. This expression of truth in conditions of despair is a constructive act.

Bacon has given a reason for preferring to paint portraits from photographs rather than in the presence of the sitter: he feels the need to injure the sitter through distortion of the images and does not want to do this in the presence of a friend. He takes chances with arbitrary marks on the canvas in the expectation that he can bring the image back from the borders of abstraction to a recognisable portrait that is more forceful and real than it could have been if more conventionally arrived at. Painting that thus takes advantage of a Surrealist idea – that the use of chance can ultimately lead to a truer reality than imitation – obviously places Bacon in a different realist category from other painters in this exhibition, one that aims to recreate the truth of existence at the expense of imitation.

There is an interesting comparison with Lucian Freud, who has pursued the human figure with the same urgency as Bacon over the same period, producing images that are equally intense. Freud has not ventured into the Surrealist use of accident but stayed within a more traditional definition of figure painting, setting himself a task – reconstructing his image through the most exacting scrutiny – that is no less testing in its own way than Bacon's. While Bacon's huge tortured images recall baroque expressions, modern secular equivalents for seventeenth-century altarpieces, Freud's vibrant but less expansive designs suggest an earlier period. Bacon's compositions keep their distance from the spectator, and seem in no way dependent on, or responsive to, the presence of an audience. But Freud's subjects occupy so much of what is generally a much smaller picture surface that there is often little or no interior space within the picture, no sense is created of a figure in its own environment, and the whole force of the design is thrown into an immediate relationship between the sitter and the artist or spectator. The sensation of closeness is further increased, especially in the early paintings, by the great size of the sitters' eyes. There is a search for communication but a denial of it at the same time, because the sitter often avoids precise eye contact. Like Bacon, Freud likes to paint people he knows well. He is unlike Bacon in needing their presence as he works.

Freud's portraits have been compared with the German Neue Sachlichkeit. In the sense of being objective or impartial Freud's pictures could almost be said to fit that description better than most of the German art of the 1920s to which it is applied. The Neue Sachlichkeit painters had the objectivity of artists who were often interested in a photographic basis for their work, but they were also preoccupied with the expression of style itself, personality and character realised through clothes, make-up and physique. Freud is different, individualising his sitters by means of minute attention to physiognomy, which is objective, rather than by the kind of personal expression through gesture or dress that would, in effect, empower the sitter to set the terms for the painting rather than the artist. It is a matter of control, which with Freud remains the prerogative of the painter.

It is possible, also, to make comparisons between Freud, especially his early painting, and the Pre-Raphaelites whose hypnotic intensity he shares. But Freud's art is more definite; he works his way over the bone structure and folds of skin on a face for signs of specific character and mood. The searching nature of painting is something to be taken literally. It is almost possible to follow in the brushwork the course of the painter's gaze as it traces its way over the sitter's features. The result is cartographical, parallel to the sense given in a rare early landscape, *Loch Ness from Drumnadrochit* 1943, which permits the viewer to follow his way across fields from stone to stone, tree to tree, hedge to hedge. In the later nudes Freud pointedly does not pose his models, but paints their splayed bodies with painstaking precision, always maintaining the feeling of physical closeness as he works. The result can be a frightening sense of the model's vulnerability, increased by the high viewpoint giving the spectator a feeling of power. The term realism as applied to Freud's painting expresses ideas about physical closeness, narrowing the gap between artist and model and offering the viewer a kind of possession, although not that implied by the idea of embrace or uncritical acceptance.

Freud's place in an exhibition about realism is clear enough. But there are other artists, like Bomberg and Auerbach, whose work has the same intensity but not the mimetic character of Freud's. Realism needs to be redefined for these artists. In his lifetime Bomberg was a detached figure in British art painting, often abroad, whose canvases were badly received by critics and public. Bomberg fitted into no artistic circle between his striking success as a Vorticist in 1914 and the very different situation some forty years later when young painters such as Auerbach and Kossoff found inspiration in his teaching. Bomberg's reputation followed a course from tentative revival in the late 1950s and early 1960s (largely due to the efforts of Marlborough

Lucian Freud *Loch Ness from Drumnadrochit* 1943

Fine Art, which looked after the reputations of many of the artists in this exhibition – Bacon, Auerbach, Kossoff and Freud as well as Bomberg – in the 1960s when Pop art and abstraction made painterly figuration unfashionable), to the mid-1970s when a kind of artistic *rappel à l'ordre* challenged conceptualism and formed itself round the notion of the School of London.

A definition of realism appropriate to Bomberg must be related to Bomberg's sense of the tactile which he first learned from the drawing master at the Slade, John Fothergill, and spent a lifetime working out.[15] Fothergill taught that drawing was not mimetic and regarded the drawn outline as having no correspondence in reality. Objects could not be known by vision alone, but were to be understood through touch. Fothergill intended the word touch literally, knowing through the experience of feeling. He also stressed the importance of accumulated experience, of the way our understanding of form is conditioned by a lifetime of learning about objects from touching them, and how, from the store of knowledge gained, the form of something can be comprehended that has not been experienced tactilely but resembles under the effects of light what has. Vision remains important but the tactile sense is primary. Referring to Bomberg's landscapes, David Sylvester has written: 'It is as if the painter, in contemplating the landscape out there, had felt he was feeling his way over it with his hands and feet and knees. It was as if the contact was so close that the painter had gone beyond being in the landscape and become the landscape.'[16] In Bomberg's painting felt experience is recreated with a remarkable nervous intensity, but it is also a constructive art, in the sense that the phrase might be used of Cézanne: Bomberg's well-practised understanding of pictorial logic made it possible for him to find rapidly the right painterly equivalent for external sensations. His canvases are not representations of things looked at from a distance, but the world brought, as it is in Freud's portraits, so close to us that we can share the artist's search. The brushmarks that characterise the work of Bomberg and his onetime students, Kossoff and Auerbach, can be seen in several ways: as aiding description, as implying movement and change, and as material substance – metaphor, possibly, for earth or flesh.

In the case of all three artists, wanting to be close to their subjects and to avoid the sense that a painting is a window onto another world by identifying subject and painting as intimately as possible is a search for possession: not possession as an exercise of power but as the counterpart to loss. In Kossoff's portraits and figure groups, for example, the sense – notwithstanding the great size and presence of the figures – that the artist is trying to anchor something tenuous and fleeting is very strong. His models are powerful and impressive, yet vulnerable at the same time. Though Kossoff is a dedicated draughtsman from the model, his figures sometimes have the apparitional character of images from memory caught and locked into the paint to give them permanence. The sense of capturing images before they escape is also present in Kossoff's urban landscapes such as the group that shows the façade and booking hall of Kilburn Underground station, a subject which itself expresses an idea of temporariness, of passing through and not belonging. There is a sense of a frustrated search for permanence and roots in the city environment which Kossoff has described thus: 'The strange ever changing light, the endless streets and the sudden feel of the sprawling city linger in my mind like a faintly glimmering memory of a long-forgotten, perhaps never experienced childhood which, if rediscovered and illuminated, would ameliorate the pain of the present.'[16]

As urban landscape painters Auerbach and Kossoff inherit Sickert's mantle. They are painters of a London that is 'real' in the sense that it is not the London of tourists and famous monuments, and is private, like Sickert's Camden Town, in the sense that its meaning stems from personal association. Like Sickert's paintings, theirs seems to belong in groups, with subjects and places repeatedly returned to, and with all three there is a feeling that they are searching for the myth of a place, something beyond mere lineaments, akin more to the character that human activity and use put on a place over a long period. Perhaps significantly none of the artists in this exhibition who have painted London (including also Bomberg and occasionally Freud) are of English parentage.

Auerbach and Kossoff exhibited drawings together at the Beaux Arts Gallery as early as 1952 and had one-man shows there in 1956 and 1957. These were the years of Bacon's growing reputation, culminating in his first Tate retrospective in 1962, and preceded the slow progress of Bomberg's recognition. The subsequent history of abstract and conceptual art slowed up and obscured the reception and popularity of several of the artists in this exhibition. 1972, the date of Kossoff's show at Whitechapel, and 1974 when Freud had his first retrospective at the Hayward, were markers, and were followed by Kitaj's use of the phrase 'School of London' in the catalogue of his exhibition The Human Clay at the Hayward in 1976. Whether there

exists a School of London that extends beyond loyalties and friendships is doubtful. But the fact that a tentative collective history that goes back to the late 1950s can be attached to many of the artists is important. The character of their work still relates to post-war debates concerned with moral, existential problems of personal identity more than to the issues of modernism that were central to the 1960s.

Notes

1. At the Goupil Gallery, April 1914.
2. New Age, April 1914.
3. Fortnightly Review, January 1911.
4. English Review, May 1912.
5. Bacon interviewed by David Sylvester in 1962, in David Sylvester, Interviews with Francis Bacon, London 1980, p.12.
6. The Times, 9 November 1923 and The Times, 30 October 1931.
7. In R.S.Lambert, Art in England, Harmondsworth 1938, p.102.
8. 'A Nonconformist', William Coldstream interviewed by Rodrigo Moynihan, Art and Literature, Lausanne, Spring 1965.
9. Art News, 12 May 1910.
10. Berger's criticism appeared mainly in the New Statesman between 1952 and 1959. On Bacon see New Statesman, 5 January 1952; on Moore see New Statesman, 5 November 1955; for the debate with Nicolson see New Statesman, 19 March 1955.
11. New Statesman, 3 October 1953.
12. Letter from Bratby to the Tate Gallery n.d. but August 1956, in Tate Gallery Modern British Paintings, Drawings and Sculptures, vol.1, 1964, p.73.
13. New Statesman, 5 January 1952.
14. Bacon interviewed by David Sylvester in 1962, in Interviews, op. cit. n.5, p.8.
15. John Fothergill, 'The Principles of Teaching Drawing at the Slade School', in Fothergill, ed., The Slade School, n.d. but ?1907, pp.38-9.
16. David Sylvester, introduction to David Bomberg 1890-1957, Marlborough Fine Art, London exhibition catalogue 1964.

Lynda Checketts

From Life

Painting is about seeing and it is the quality of a painter's vision that convinces us. Ideas of depiction are handed down from painter to painter and every good painter adds something of his own to the rich vocabulary of the language of painting. The great art of the past gives painters a privileged relationship with history. As Sickert said: 'There is no such thing as modern art. There is no such thing as ancient art … History is one unbroken stream, if we know Degas, Degas knew Ingres, and so on, ad infinitum.'

The handing on of knowledge from one painter to another should not be confused with art education. Many of the artists in this exhibition have found art schools lack, and sometimes actively oppose, the passing on of a knowledge of seeing, instead they try to teach the impossible – *imagination*. Painters often teach by demonstration, showing, rather than telling.

Painting is not a nationalistic activity in the nineteenth-century sense of nationhood, although it does have a looser geographic identity which comes from practical considerations of climate and social patterns. Over half the painters in this exhibition have, in part, been shaped by other countries.

Sickert was a Dane, born in Munich. After a term at the Slade School in London he left to become Whistler's assistant and spent much of his time in France. Whistler had trained in Paris with Gleyre. In the Louvre, he met Fantin-Latour and Alphonse Legros, students of Lecoq de Boisbaudran.[1] Whistler's draughtsmanship had an enduring influence on Sickert: 'Whistler's sense of the direction of a line was acute. That sense – which is the whole art of drawing – made of him a miraculously gifted, intuitive draughtsman, and master of perspective.'[2] Sickert and Whistler always drew 'sight-size': 'In drawing a whole figure from nature we must be three times its length from it … we must draw on the scale on which we should trace, if our sheet of paper were a sheet of glass.'[3] Sickert also emphasised the efficiency of working sight-size: 'Obviously the person who draws on the scale of vision is performing a simpler operation than one who either reduces or enlarges what he sees.'[4]

Whistler painted with a restricted palette, often using only tones of grey and black. He concentrated on 'the unity of vision',[5] the way in which the quality of light falling on the painter's subject creates a harmony and unity between all the objects, and the space in which they exist. It is the fleeting quality of light that a painter depicts. This was the quality of Venetian painting in the sixteenth century which influenced Velázquez in Spain in the seventeenth century who in turn was admired by French painters in the nineteenth century. 'The acute direction of a line' and the 'unity of vision' influenced all Sickert's

work, but he also questioned: '… why then did he [Whistler] incur endless and futile sittings for works which, far from ripening under his brush, became from lively infants that they were, wrecks of ghosts of ghosts. The great painters painted from drawings that remained stable, and not in the presence of the "movie" that is nature.'[6]

From 1885 Sickert spent his summers in Dieppe, with the artists who met at the studio of Jacques Emile Blanche, who included Degas. A difference between Degas and the realists is illustrated by Camille Pissarro's response to his son's decision to study with Legros at the Slade School in London: 'Osny, June 13, 1883, My dear Lucien; I mentioned to Degas that you are thinking of taking Legros' course in drawing. Degas says that there is one way of escaping Legros' influence, the method is simply this: it is to reproduce, in your own place, from memory, the drawing you made in class … the observations you make from memory will have far more power and be much more original … The drawing will have art – it will be your own.'[7]

Degas drew from nature and painted from drawings and from memory recreating the surprise of a fleeting moment. Degas encouraged Sickert to draw swiftly and to discover beauty in his own time and place. For the music hall paintings, Sickert returned night after night to the same seat in the theatre, making many studies which he then pieced together in a final compositional drawing for a painting.[8] Some of Sickert's drawings combine layers of marks in pencil, chalk and pen and ink, to distinguish different tones in the painting.

Sickert made four visits to Venice, in 1895-6, 1900, 1901 and 1903-4, attracted by the city and most of all by the light in Venetian painting. In Titian he found the 'unity of vision'. Sickert's views of Venice are remarkable for their economy. The entire surface of the canvas was dashed in, layer by layer, allowing each to dry before applying the next. From a mid tone he tended to work into the shadows and then the light tones, keeping the painting open, always allowing changes to the drawing and tone. This parallels Titian's mature technique,[9] so strikingly seen in the unrestored *Flaying of Marsyas* (in *The Genius of Venice* exhibition at the Royal Academy in 1983). Early Flemish oil paintings were painted from light to dark. Giorgione and Titian reversed this process, to work from dark to light as a means of unifying their vision, which was quite different from the 'clarity of vision' of the Northern Renaissance.

Sickert's final visit to Venice in 1903-4 resulted in a number of very beautiful interior portraits. In *Mamma Mia Poveretta* 1903-4 (**1**) the brushmarks, the lighting and the dignified pose of the tough old lady foreshadow the domestic dramas of the Camden Town period and the paintings of *Hubby and Marie c.* 1912 (**3**).

When Sickert returned to London he claimed he had found a way of teaching painting that would enable anyone to paint competent pictures. These ideas can be found in his writings.[10] He painted from drawings, squared up the drawings for exact transfer to a canvas of the same proportions, and he worked on a mid tone ground, drawing with the brush, keeping in every mark including accidents. A mark in a drawing relates exactly to a brushmark in the painting.

His teaching was a focus for the young painters who became known as the Camden Town Group; Gore and Gilman, who had previously studied at the Slade School under Fred Brown and Henry Tonks, and Ginner. The accounts of Tonks' teaching of drawing at the Slade emphasise 'form' expressed by outline or contour and by light and shade. Drawings were made in front of the object and sight-size. Tonks believed the 'imaginative' element in art is formed by the artist's character: '...so it is not in the power of the drawing master to teach it'. It is through touch and motion that we learn to interpret the flat patterns received by the retina of the eye. The depiction of form, the art of drawing, was for Tonks the depiction of the draughtsman's 'idea of touch'. Not all drawing was art, he distinguished symbolic from pure drawing: symbolic drawing is used to tell a story and its value is its meaning: 'pure drawing has a content that cannot be expressed in words, that content is form'.[11]

Tonks' emphasis on form as contour and outline led his students to work with Florentine clarity. Stanley Spencer's pictures were all organised in a manner he initially worked out for Slade Summer Compositions. Tonks' admiration for the Italian Quattrocento probably encouraged Spencer's interest in murals. Spencer transferred squared up compositional drawings, painting meticulously square by square. His landscapes and some portraits were painted from life. The perspective of *Cottages at Burghclere* 1930-1 (**20**) has two vanishing points, at either side of the central house, to cope with the panoramic view.

Teaching at the Slade about 1946, Spencer drew a demonstration portrait for the students. He began with one eye and then worked across the forehead before completing the second eye. By that time the model was asleep, so the drawing had one eye open and the other closed.[12] It is Spencer's curious, but logical, way of working that gives such intensity to his paintings, and this is most apparent in his nude portraits of his two wives. The Life Room at the Slade must have been an extraordinary place for the adolescent Spencer. He said years later: 'I never had professional models, not liking the idea.' The Patricia Preece nudes were probably painted both from drawings and from life. Viewed vertically her resting head in *Self-Portrait with Patricia Preece* 1936 (**21**) is a painful grimace. The very beautiful, straightforward painting of Hilda, *Seated Nude* 1942 (**24**), was painted from a drawing made twelve or thirteen years earlier.

Tonks was concerned that Roger Fry's and Clive Bell's enthusiasm for pattern, decoration and primitive qualities in Post-Impressionist painting, would 'take art off the Gold Standard' by divorcing drawing and painting from the study of life. Fry promoted Cézanne as 'a painter of abstract values' who, according to Maurice Denis, '...is nearer to that of a Persian Carpet Weaver than of a Delacroix'.[13] David Bom-

Cézanne *Bathers* c. 1895-1904

berg and William Coldstream were both influenced by Fry while at the Slade. The conflict of values caused crises in their painting. Both resolved these doubts through Sickert's influence. Sickert was wary of the ideas Maurice Denis represented. Sickert's knowledge of Degas and his circle provided him with a much broader understanding of modern French painting.

Bomberg said his paintings and drawings had a 'Degas-Sickert affinity' in 1908-10. He attended Sickert's life classes at the Westminster School of Art, for two years before he went to the Slade.[14] Like Coldstream, Bomberg broke with Cubism but retained an immense admiration for Cézanne, who he felt was a perceptual painter the Cubists had misunderstood and had attempted to mechanise. There is a continuity in the depiction of movement between Bomberg's Cubist paintings and his later perceptual pictures. The drawing *Study for The South East Corner, Jerusalem* 1926 is squared up for transfer to a canvas, another drawing of Jerusalem appears to have been traced on glass. The rapid painting of Jerusalem by moonlight, *Mount Zion with the Church of the Dormition: Moonlight* 1923 (**11**) is painted from nature, *alla prima*, in a single session. Bomberg drew with the paint brush, finally fixing the detail in the lightest and darkest tones, laid thickly over large areas of paint, blended wet into wet. The whole scene is there in the blocks of colour and brushmarks which give a strong and direct equivalent of reality. The underlying structure of the painting is the precision with which Bomberg drew. He drew with the brush in the way Sickert advocated, but he did not usually paint directly from drawings. He drew to gain knowledge of a subject and intimacy with it and they were ends in themselves. His paintings were made directly from nature with a sense of urgency, to paint his vision before it faded.

Evening in the City of London 1944 (**17**), is Bomberg's masterpiece of war-torn London, crowned by the blackened silhouette of St Paul's. The colour is hot but subdued, with white turning the reds to pink and the browns to plum, in a fusion of a sunset and the Blitz. Lilian Bomberg recalled: 'He got permission to climb to the top of a church, in Cheapside I think, and painted St Paul's from its east side … it was done in one go, but he did the drawing for it first.'[15]

On Tonks' advice, Coldstream attended lectures given by Sickert in 1929 at the Royal Institution. He remembered : 'Sickert said "When you begin a drawing, you want to look at one particular spot on the drawing and identify it – and then you say, does the line (as far as there is a line), does it go North or South or East or West".'[16] Coldstream valued Cézanne as a continuation of the tradition of painting from nature, rather than the beginning of Cubism. In 1934 Coldstream turned to film-making with the GPO Film Unit. He was joined there in 1935 by W. H. Auden who encouraged him to return to painting. Auden's poem 'Letter to William Coldstream, Esq.'[17] hinges on the painter's idea of 'the impersonal eye of the camera', perhaps the origin of Christopher Isherwood's 'I am a camera with its shutter open'. In 1936 and 1937 Coldstream painted portraits from life of Auden's mother and the three poets Isherwood, Auden and Stephen Spender. The Spender portrait (**27**) is superb. The clarity of the drawing, around the eye socket and cheek, remind one of Cranach.

To earn a living during the Depression Claude Rogers opened the Euston Road School with Coldstream, Graham Bell and Victor Pasmore. The prospectus announced : 'Instruction will be given in drawing and painting from life : the head and the figure, still life and landscape, and in making paintings from drawings …'[18] Coldstream did not paint from drawings[19] but Graham Bell did. In 1938 Sickert gave a lecture at the Euston Road School, and he stressed he always painted from drawings and, at that time, also from photographs. Victor Pasmore asked if he had ever worked from nature to which Sickert replied : 'Not since I was grown up'.[20]

A bridge between the early part of the century and post-war figurative artists is formed by Bomberg, Coldstream and Helen Lessore. At the Beaux Arts Gallery from 1951 to 1965 she organised the first exhibitions of Michael Andrews, Frank Auerbach, Leon Kossoff, John Lessore, Euan Uglow, and many other of our most respected figurative artists. She had studied with Tonks at the Slade from 1924 to 1928. Her husband, Frederick Lessore, the sculptor, had studied with Rodin, and was the brother of Thérèse Lessore, Sickert's wife. Helen Lessore wrote two articles on Sickert's late paintings, 'English Echoes', which were based on mid-Victorian illustrations.[21] Sickert used other people's drawings and photographs for many of his late paintings. The curious juxtaposition of Victorian illustration and photography represents the profound change that took place in the popular language of depiction during his lifetime. The paintings based on photographs include *High Steppers* c. 1938-9 (**8**) and *Alexander Gavin Henderson, 2nd Lord Faringdon* (**9**). In *The Temple Bar* c. 1941 (**10**), he kept the grid of squares he had used to transfer the engraving to the canvas, emphasising their abstract necessity. The paint is scumbled across the hessian, as it is in Titian's late work. Auerbach has seen a drawing of Sickert's actually cut up into these squares so it could be transferred without reference to the complete image.[22]

A number of the young painters Helen Lessore found to exhibit at the Beaux Arts Gallery had studied with either Bomberg or Coldstream. Her paintings *Symposium I & II* 1974-7 and 1974-83, are

Helen Lessore *Symposium I* 1974-7

compositions of a gathering of the artists she cares most about. At the head of the table is Francis Bacon. In *A Partial Testament*, Helen Lessore called Bacon the painter '… most firmly rooted in the great European tradition'. Next to him sits Lucian Freud. Freud's early paintings, such as the portrait *Francis Bacon* 1952 and the 1951 *Girl with Beret* (**49**), show his natural inclination towards the linear in early German and Flemish painting. Every eye-lash and freckle is painted as clearly as if it has been studied under a magnifying glass. Freud is at the same time a modern painter ; the drawing of features in the early paintings sometimes derives from a subtle combination of full face and profile.

By the late 1950s Freud had begun a difficult search for a broader method of painting. The change was influenced by the painters he was looking at closely, Rembrandt, Rubens and Frans Hals. The painting in *Reflection with Two Children (Self-portrait)* 1965, has been influenced by Bacon, with the children painted on an impossible scale, like donors in an Altdorfer.

The portrait of a woman in a white shirt, *Last Portrait* 1974-5, shows his method of working from the centre outwards, finishing the figure before moving on. He always paints in front of the subject and not from drawings. By the 1980s, the paint in *Two Irishmen in W.11* 1984-5 (**53**) and *Naked Girl with Egg* 1980-1 (**52**) has become thick, leaving streaks from the hog's hair brush. The floor and parts of the furniture are painted *alla prima* with the colours mingling together, but his paint seldom crosses the boundaries between objects. In the marvellous nudes from 1978 and early 1982, like *Naked Girl with Egg*, the thick paint is pulled and sculpted to form what is almost a second skin of the person. The paintings are further intensified by being painted under strong electric lights, and with the painter physcially very close to the model, Freud like Spencer breaks the convention of space between people, and he brings us into intimacy with another human being.

Lucian Freud *Large Interior W.11 (after Watteau)* 1981 - 3

Freud is restricted by his technique to subject-matter that will keep still but *The Large Interior, W.11 (after Watteau)* 1981 - 3 and *Painter and Model* 1986 - 7 (**55**) show his ability to paint relationships on an ambitious scale while maintaining the intense interior drama of his earlier work. The emphasis on the single figure was a preoccupation of many painters just after the war. Isolation is the dominant image of Existentialism and of Giacometti who was an enormous influence. David Sylvester has suggested that the sculptures Giacometti gave to the Tate Gallery were a direct result of the two retrospective exhibitions of his work in London which Coldstream had encouraged.

Just after the war Coldstream painted *The Rt Hon The Earl Jowitt* 1947 - 51, and around the same time he wrote in an essay on Holbein's

Alberto Giacometti *Diego* 1959

William Coldstream *The Rt Hon The Earl Jowitt* 1947-51

Ambassadors: 'What struck me most about the Ambassadors was its magnificent decorative quality ... firmly cut into a tremendously arresting pattern of flat shapes ... in the Holbein picture we know the solid shape of the objects represented because of the accuracy of their outline.'[23] This idea of the flat canvas comes from his interest in Matisse: 'I had a very strong feeling that the flat surface of the painting was extremely beautiful, and the more you did to it the better, providing that you did not break it.'

Euan Uglow was a student of Coldstream at Camberwell and the Slade from 1948 to 1954. Uglow employs the mathematics of rectangles to create a tension in his paintings between the surface geometry and the model, and he respects the flatness of the picture surface. The paintings remind one that it is not really an eye you are looking at, but a mark in the right position for an eye.

For the *Nude, from Twelve Regular Vertical Positions from the Eye* 1967 (**67**) he built a mechanism on which he could move himself physically up or down the figure to twelve predetermined positions. He was then measuring 5 or 6 inches rather than 5 or 6 feet. As the measurements progressed the painting stretched to 8 feet because of the gaps which

appeared where the model was farthest from his eye, because his measurements did not join up, and in this way he paralleled the thinness of Giacometti's sculptures.

Uglow spends a long time searching for the position and proportion of the model within a rectangle. His paintings are worked on from the centre out, and the edge and hence the size of the picture are only determined some time into the painting. He always works in front of the model, measuring bit by bit, finding and comparing equal distances in his view of his model and equivalents on the surface of the canvas. A model may need to pose for fifty sessions or more. He is interested in the largeness of the part of the model closest to him and the smallness of the part farthest away, as in the elegant narrow shoulders and broad thighs and knees of the model in *Celebration of the New Skylight* 1986-7 (**70**). The central division in the painting runs through the model's right eye to the peak of the dark mountain shape between her thighs. The colour is clear and precise from the pure white highlights to her glowing orange belly, set off by the complementary green measurement marks. Uglow paints the white walls of his studio green-grey revealing the colour in the light and shadow on the white walls of a gallery where the painting may hang.

Looking at the painting one is reminded of Cézanne's simple equation: 'The more the colour harmonises the more the drawing becomes precise. When the colour has attained richness, the form has reached its plenitude.' As a teacher Uglow stresses that the colours should harmonise. In his *Summer Picture* 1972 the blue wall and wooden table in the intense summer light echo the pure blue and gold of a Quattrocento fresco.

Frank Auerbach and Leon Kossoff studied at St Martin's School of Art and the Royal College of Art, and with David Bomberg whose part-time classes they attended in the late 1940s and early 1950s at the Borough Polytechnic.

Auerbach emphasises that Bomberg was a very intelligent man, a consciously pedagogic teacher, who grandly over-estimated the experience of his young students. He considered all painting was drawing and he would often repeat 'it's all drawing ... drawing is not line but mental grasp'. He taught within a tradition, emphasising 'form' and 'direction'. He used Tonks' idea of 'touch' as the representation of form and he used Sickert's analogies between the direction of a line and a map, and the 360° of a circle. When he abandoned Vorticism and Cubism after the First World War Bomberg was in effect growing out of stressing the conceptual part of a painters' language over the perceptual. He taught by demonstration and: 'by pointing out the *errors* in their drawings which he did with devastating acuity. Concrete, demonstrable errors in drawing.'[24]

Auerbach's subjects are limited, as Bomberg's were, to portraits and nudes painted from life in the studio and landscapes, also painted in the studio but using drawings made in the streets and park near his studio in Camden Town.

Auerbach has a strong work ethic: 'for a painter the problem is to go as long as possible with one work and to drive it to its most comprehensive and economical conclusion'. The spectator must also work in front of his portraits, whether the early *Head of E.O.W.* 1954 (**38**) or *Head of Catherine Lampert II* 1988 (**43**), past the look of the paint through to the person posing in front of the painter, man or woman, young or old, seated or standing, in electric light or day light: 'It seems to me that toes, ears, chair legs, fingernails must be in there somewhere even if they cannot be found in the final image.'[25] Auerbach's portraits and nudes have a great sense of space, in the midst of which is the figure. This increases the frail beauty of figures such as *E.O.W. on Her Blue Eiderdown* 1965 (**39**). 'When I taught I used to say to students – don't start a "life drawing" ask yourself what it feels like to be standing in this room, with all its contents including this amazing naked person".'[26]

Kossoff wrote down his thoughts on drawing in the catalogue of Auerbach's 1978 exhibition: 'Drawing is not a mysterious activity. Drawing is making an image which expresses commitment and involvement. This only comes about after seemingly endless activity before the model or subject, rejecting time and again ideas which are possible to preconceive. And, whether by scraping off or rubbing down, it is always beginning again, making new images, destroying images that lie, discarding images that are dead.'[27]

Kossoff draws from life, and paints from his drawings and from memory. He quotes Sickert: 'Perhaps the chief source of pleasure in the aspect of the nude is that it is in the nature of a gleam – a gleam of light and warmth and life.' His nudes are human, vulnerable and poignant. Awkwardly and simply posed they gaze out of the side of the picture, avoiding our eyes.

In all Kossoff's portraits one becomes aware that the face and body are themselves a portrait of the disposition of the person, the experience of life is the artist the painter must follow. In *Father Seated in Armchair* 1960 (**56**), he explores the surface signs of age, pitting, dragging and wrinkling the paint as he tries to comprehend ageing.

Kossoff has a strong sense of the subject, of the people and places he knows best; his parents, his wife, his brothers, a few friends and his models Pauline and Fidelma. *Christchurch, Spitalfields, Early Summer* 1987 (**60**) is a vision, like a Sassetta seen above the clouds. A back-street school is his cathedral and an Underground booking hall is his theatre. At the swimming pool a diver takes up the pose of Picasso's stretching musician. Kossoff is a modern painter in the great tradition.

Since the Renaissance drawings made from nature formed the basis from which compositions were painted. We can see this in the work of Degas, Pissarro, Seurat and Van Gogh. It continued in the practice of Bonnard, Vuillard, Sickert, Derain and Balthus but many twentieth-century figurative painters limited their subjects by working directly from life. In his early 1960s paintings Michael Andrews revived the ambition to compose complex paintings of modern life.

For *The Family in the Garden* 1960-2 (**33**), Andrews made compositional drawings but he painted the picture from nature in a temporary shelter he had built for his canvas in the garden of his parents' home in Norwich. In this way he was able to pose the figures individually, working on the painting over three summers. *The Colony Room I* 1962 (**34**) was painted in his studio in Islington, away from the subject. There is a small oil study for the painting, suggesting that he may have made studies in the club or in his studio of the central figures, as well as developing it from drawings and memory. Later in 1962 he painted *The Deer Park* from a combination of memory, other paintings, drawings and photographs.

Sickert said of the use of photographs by a painter, that 'the indulgence has some analogy to alcohol, allowable only to those who can do without it'.[28] The vision of all the painters in this exhibition has been formed in a culture permeated by the language of photography, and it has affected them all, sometimes postively as in the idea of monocular vision of Coldstream and Uglow, and sometimes critically as in the long process of rejection of preconceived images by Auerbach and Kossoff. Bacon does not make drawings and uses photographs including reproductions of paintings, film stills, illustrations from medical text books and portrait photographs. The small heads Andrews painted in the late 1960s for *The Lord Mayor's Reception in Norwich Castle* were made on top of photographs printed on a light-sensitive linen called Turaphot.[29] He used photography in the rôle of drawing and he learnt to combine photographs and paintings in a linear and flat technique which had the compensation of entirely freeing his subject-matter. By the late 1970s his paint had become looser but still

Michael Andrews *Melanie and Me Swimming* 1978-9

clear, showing his delight in formalised patterns. In a great image of a father's love for his daughter, *Melanie and Me Swimming* 1978-9 he has found a way of painting from photographs that has the grace of Vermeer's use of a camera obscura.

Andrews has used the visual language of photographs without carrying over the dated quality photographs soon acquire. All his paintings are concerned with the creation of a visual language that is a convincing depiction of the feeling of the present-day world.

John Wonnacott remembers going to Cookham with some school friends in the early 1950s to meet Stanley Spencer. His next visit was to Florence to see Masaccio's Trinity. He entered the Slade in 1958 and was taught by Frank Auerbach and, for a term, by Michael Andrews. His early paintings show his debt to Auerbach. He has written that: 'My aim was to construct, through a wrestling by trial and error with the materials, an image intense enough to be matched against the presence of the "real" seen object.'[30]

Michael Andrews' exhibition at the Beaux Arts Gallery in January 1963 had a powerful impact on him. The idea of composition in Andrews' *The Family in the Garden* 1960-2 (**33**) inspired his *The Family* 1963-74, a painting of light and space about growing up, growing old and death. In his final year at the Slade, Wonnacott began to relate the formal mechanics of painting to the way an eye sees. He emphasises 'you do not learn to draw, you learn to understand how you see'. The *Family* documents the distortions which occurred at the edge of a field of vision. The field of vision is usually about 90°, but

Wonnacott extended the painting during the eleven years he worked on it to an angle of vision of nearly 180°.

The mechanics of seeing led to the *Window* paintings, which literally demonstrate the idea of tracing on a pane of glass. In these paintings he gained the technical confidence to paint ambitious subjects, which eventually led to the grand *Portrait of Sir Adam Thomson* 1985-6 (**74**) of British Caledonian, commissioned by the Scottish National Portrait Gallery, and set beneath the colossal metal web of an aircraft hangar. A perfect modern subject for the representation of three-dimensional space by the two-dimensional geometry of perspective.

Wonnacott regularly returns to painting small individual portraits from life, as a means of refreshing his keen sense of reality. The space of the small paintings, such as the *Self-Portrait* 1988-9, contrasts with the wide angle of vision of his large pictures, and enables him to intensify his colour. I sat for my portrait *Lynda* twice a week from 1982 to 1984. He made a number of drawings at the beginning and at different stages in the painting and he took photographs of the pose. He also worked on the painting in his own time and repainted the entire picture more than once to retrieve his memory of the nuances of light in his original vision.

John Wonnacott taught with John Lessore in the Life Room at Norwich School of Art from 1978 to 1986. In *The Life Room, Norwich School of Art* 1980-1, John Lessore places the model in the foreground. Gathered round her are the students on 'donkeys', their heads tilted with earnest, silent concentration and beyond are two plaster casts, *Dionysus* and the *Discophoros*. In the distance is John Wonnacott painting *The Life Room* 1977-80. In Wonnacott's painting the view is reversed with the model at the far end of the room and Lessore's painting is in progress. The difference in atmosphere is enormous. Wonnacott's space is convex where Lessore's is concave.

The *Norwich School of Art* 1982-4 (**73**) by Wonnacott and *The Garth* 1982-3 (**64**) by Lessore, show the front and courtyard of the same building. Lessore has turned his students into a triumphal procession of children. Holding their rulers like candles they are transformed into Quattrocento angels. Wonnacott's figures reflect the politics of the School at the time.[31] He paints exactly what one sees walking up to the bridge in St George Street. Like Spencer's *Cottages at Burghclere* c.1930-1 (**20**) the painting is organised round two vanishing points, one behind the Cathedral, the other at the top of the street. The two view points diverge, subtly creating the forward thrust of the School building.

The difference between Wonnacott and Lessore's paintings is typical of the contrast between the 'clarity of vision' of the Northern tradition, and the 'unity of vision' of Southern European painting. Wonnacott's vision is 'a direct confrontation with appearances'[32] and contrasts with Lessore's belief that the convincing presence of the final image is more important than the visual appearance of the original subject. Among Lessore's earliest memories are the sombre tones and colours of war-damaged London and he still feels for the old and worn as something comfortable.

In 1986 John Lessore wrote: 'Men and women are the central subject matter of all great visual art, and this is true of virtually all civilisa-

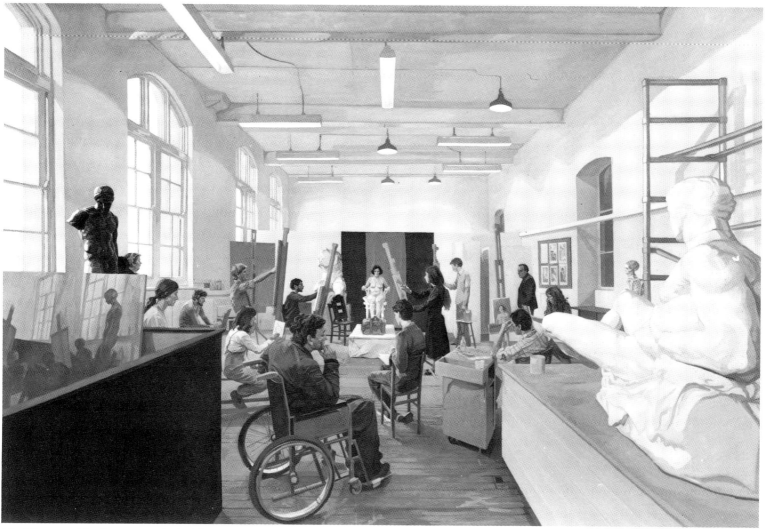

John Wonnacott *The Life Room, Norwich School of Art* 1977 - 80

tions from the earliest times and the most primitive conditions. The most beautiful, mysterious and inexhaustible subject is the human body and the human head. My chief interest in landscape and architecture is as a setting for mankind. I believe the patterns of growth and proportion in man and nature to be the basis of architecture.'[33]

At the Slade he was influenced by Thomas Monnington who he considers was one of the most naturally gifted draughtsmen of this century. Taught by Tonks, he drew according to the Florentine tradition, exploring three-dimensional shapes with great attention to their flow and rhythm: a quite different approach from Coldstream's vision with its network of marks and measurement.

Most of Lessore's compositions are based on drawings; he paints from drawings and memory as well as from life. As a draughtsman his priorities are movement and volume, but when painting, he also strives for a tonal unity which will involve endless adjustments until he feels he has achieved a true pitch for every inch of the picture.

In 1958 and 1959 he posed for Leon Kossoff for the painting *Man*

in a Wheelchair now in the Tate Gallery and their friendship has continued. His painting *Artist and Model I* 1988 - 9 (**65**) is one of a series of paintings of Kossoff, begun soon after his first visit to the Prado in 1986. They explore the myth of artist and model and are haunted by Kossoff's paintings of Kilburn Underground. The large Kossoff painting in the background of *Artist and Model* acts as if it were a tapestry. With subtle ambiguity painted figures become real presences, entering the same world as their painted creator while the model dozes in the glow of an electirc fire. Throughout the series the proportions of the room vary; the light changes; the colour harmony moves from green to brown, grey or blue and the only constant is Lessore's homage to the heroic art of painting from life.

Kossoff stands to work, leaning his board against a chair back, or cans of paint. His paint brushes are the size of tulip buds. Under the windows and in the corners are great mounds of scraped off paint, paper and rags. He works with the curtains drawn across the windows. Here we see labour and intellect, materials and subject-

Leon Kossoff *Man in a Wheelchair* 1959-62

Notes

1. Lecoq de Boisbaudran published an influential book, *The Training of the Visual Memory for Artists*, translated by Selwyn Image and Lowes Dalbiac Luard, c.1910.
2. Letter to *The Times*, 12 July 1934. Quoted in *Walter Richard Sickert: Advice to Young Artists*, ed. by Lynda Morris, Norwich School of Art Gallery exhibition catalogue, 1986.
3. 'The Study of Drawing' by Sickert, *The New Age*, 16 June 1910. Quoted in *Advice to Young Artists*, op. cit. n.2.
4. 'The Whitworth Art Gallery' by Sickert, *The Manchester Guardian*, 9 March 1926. Quoted in *Advice to Young Artists*, op. cit. n.2.
5. Philip Wilson Steer, 'Impressionism in Art', Lecture to the Art Workers Guild 1891. Reprinted in *Philip Wilson Steer*, D.S.MacColl, London 1945. Steer used the term as the basis of Impressionism and the constant factor in all good painting. Steer and Sickert were founder-members in 1889 of the 'London Impressionists', which became the New English Art Club.
6. *Advice to Young Artists*, op. cit. n.2.
7. *Camille Pissarro, Letters to his Son Lucien*, edited by John Rewald, London, 4th ed. 1980.
8. 'Sickert Drawings' by Gabriel White, *Image* 7, Spring 1952.
9. There is an account of Titian's mature technique and a record of a visit to his studio in *Vasari's Lives of the Artists*, translated by George Bull, Harmondsworth 1965.
10. *A Free House! or The Artist as Craftsman: The Writings of Walter Richard Sickert*, edited by Osbert Sitwell, London 1947. *Advice to Young Artists*, op. cit. n.2.
11. *Elementary Propositions in Drawing and Painting*, Henry Tonks and George Clausen, Girls Public Day School Trust 1910. Reprinted in *Henry Tonks and the Art of Pure Drawing*, edited by Lynda Morris, Norwich School of Art Gallery 1985. 'The Principles of Teaching Drawing at the Slade', John Fothergill, *The Slade*, published privately 1907. 'Drawing', Fothergill, *Encyclopaedia Britannica* 1910-11.
12. Dorothy Ransome who attended Spencer's classes, in conversation with the author 1989.
13. 'Cézanne', Maurice Denis translated and introduced by Roger Fry, *Burlington Magazine*, January 1910 pp.207-19 and February 1910, pp.275-80.
14. He said his paintings and drawings had a 'Degas-Sickert affinity' when he was first interviewed for the Slade in 1909. Unpublished writings by Bomberg. Quoted in Richard Cork, *David Bomberg*, New Haven and London 1987, p.15.
15. Lilian Bomberg in an interview with Richard Cork 1981, ibid. p.254.
16. 'Coldstream and Representational Painting', Lynda Morris, *Art Monthly*, September 1984, from an unpublished transcript of a tape recording of a debate on 'Like' held at the Slade in 1976. The debate was chaired by David Sylvester and included Lucian Freud, Euan Uglow and Coldstream.
17. *Letters from Iceland*, W.H. Auden and Louis MacNeice, London 1937, repr.1967.
18. Quoted in *English Art and Modernism 1900 to 1939*, London and Bloomington, Indiana 1981.
19. Artist's Statement, *The Tate Gallery Catalogue of Acquisitions 1968-9*.
20. Duncan Grant on a Sickert Lecture', Richard Shone, *Burlington Magazine*, November 1981, pp. 671-2.
21. Née Helen Brook. *The Studio*, May 1932, pp. 266-71. This is the collective title given to the pictures by Helen Lessore; the Arts Council *Late Sickert* exhibition, 1981 called them 'Echoes'.
22. Review of Wendy Baron's *Sickert* by Frank Auerbach, *The Listener*, 14 June 1973.
23. 'Holbein', William Coldstream, *The Listener*, 5 February 1947, p.239, first broadcast on the BBC Third Programme.
24. From a questionnaire Auerbach completed for an unpublished dissertation on Bomberg's Teaching, Neil MacGregor, Norwich School of Art 1985.
25. Ibid.
26. Ibid.
27. Leon Kossoff, 'The Paintings of Frank Auerbach', in *Frank Auerbach*, Hayward Gallery, London exhibition catalogue 1978.
28. *Advice to Young Artists*, op. cit. n.2.
29. Andrews devised the method with Nigel Henderson at Norwich School of Art.
30. 'Artist's Statement', *John Wonnacott: Paintings and Drawings*, Rochdale Art Gallery exhibition catalogue 1978.
31. See the entry in *The Tate Gallery Catalogue of Acquisitions 1986-8*.
32. 'Artist's Statement', op. cit. n.30.
33. Unpublished notes for an interview with John Wonnacott and John Lessore on their teaching in the Life Room at Norwich School of Art by Lynda Morris 1986.

matter, locked in an endless struggle to make permanent the magic of the vanishing instant. It is the artist in thrall to the beauty he sees in life.

But, for the spectator it is life enhanced by art, that amazes. As Manuel Chrysoloras wrote in his great humanist letter of 1411 describing his feelings in front of the rediscovered marvels of Classical Greece: '... we admire not so much the beauty of the bodies in statues and paintings, as the beauty of the mind of their maker'.

Michael Peppiatt

The School of London in Europe

Both concepts announced in the title of this essay stand for an unruly, fluctuating reality, but the notion that a 'School of London' actually exists has now gained considerable support. The phrase was used to designate a section of the Royal Academy's *British Art in the 20th Century*, and it was the theme of an exhibition entitled *A School of London* that toured Europe in 1987.[1] Since then, as always happens with such handy appellations, it has been stretched to include an intriguing, even bewildering variety of other artists at work in England. Before further commentators blur the outlines and the *raison d'être* of the original concept, it would be useful to redefine the criteria that allow us to see these artists as a group.

For a 'school' of artists of any kind to emerge in a period that has been as committed as ours to a belief in individual, not to say isolated, creativity is improbable; and in London all the more so, since English artists have been notoriously reluctant to form groups and movements. A glance at the painters brought together under this banner confirms the apparent contradiction. If Francis Bacon, Lucian Freud, Leon Kossoff, Michael Andrews and Frank Auerbach have one characteristic in common, after all, it is their innate, fiercely preserved sense of individuality.

Yet imprecise and awkward as it is, the 'School of London' phrase sticks, because it communicates a fact for which no other formula has been found. It means, in essence, that over the past forty years a body of work has evolved in London which possesses a power and a relevance to the future of painting that would be hard to match anywhere else in the world. This contention may seem less partial and indeed begin to take on its real, international significance once one adds that it was first put forward by the American-born painter and longtime London resident, R. B. Kitaj.

The phrase originally occurred in the preface for a show of contemporary figure painting that Kitaj had organised. 'The bottom line is that there are artistic personalities in this small island more unique and strong and I think numerous than anywhere in the world outside America's jolting artistic vigour ... If some of the strange and fascinating personalities you may encounter here were given a fraction of the attention and encouragement reserved in this barren time for provincial and orthodox vanguardism', he wrote, 'a School of London might become even more real than the one I have construed in my head ... with potent art lessons for foreigners emerging from this odd old, put upon, very singular place.'[2]

Used loosely, School of London would indeed become as vague, all-embracing a term as École de Paris, particularly given the range of talented figurative painters to have emerged in England. But at the centre – one might say, at the source – of the renewal of interest in the human figure as painting's 'proper study', there is a 'hard core' of artists whose inventiveness and dedication to the figurative image, notably throughout the heyday of abstraction, give them the stature and authority of trailblazers.

Obsessive fascination with the figure as the subject through which the most profound feelings about human existence can be conveyed, as well as a parallel disregard for the fluctuations of artistic fashion, have linked the five artists under discussion from early on in their careers. Not only their work but their lives have been closely interrelated, as the frequent portraits they have done of each other suggest. They have shared galleries and appeared frequently in the same group shows. They have followed one another's development keenly – sometimes critically, but never without a personal involvement, as if each one had something at stake in the others' art. Though they tend to be highly private, even reclusive, individuals, they have talked or argued together at length; and their artistic outlook has to some extent been shaped by those discussions.

In these respects, and in the many artistic and literary admirations they have in common, the School of London painters could be considered as closely knit as the Impressionists. Like the Impressionists, they adhere to no particular programme, but there is probably more to connect Bacon with Freud than Manet with Monet, while Auerbach and Kossoff have greater affinities in outlook, working methods and style than any two of their French predecessors.[3] As Auerbach has pointed out, 'artists usually come in gangs', and, more recently, when asked what he thought about the School of London idea, he said: 'It may be that there has been a slightly more gritty and determined and personal engagement with the physical world in London than there has been in some other places – that artists here have actually felt it exciting and interesting and new to record their physical situation.'[4] Despite their manifest individuality of vision, this particular 'gang' has also drawn a great deal of common identity from having shared the same urban milieu.

London has provided a continuous backdrop to the development of these artists, except for Michael Andrews, who left the capital for the seclusion of his native Norfolk over a decade ago. But although they have all been deeply affected by the city, only Kossoff is London-born. Freud and Auerbach both came as young children to England from Berlin, while Bacon was born in Dublin and Michael Andrews in Norwich. The disinherited vision of the city they convey is as central to their work as post-war Paris was to Sartre or Giacometti; and the atmosphere of guilt and human vulnerability that seeps out

L-R: Timothy Behrens, Lucian Freud, Francis Bacon, Frank Auerbach, and
Michael Andrews at Wheeler's restaurant, Old Compton Street, London 1962

of their pictures constantly recalls the Existentialist mood.

A true Cockney, Leon Kossoff has long conducted a sumptuous and
melancholy celebration of the city. His pictures are run through with
a poetry of ordinariness: the sag of ill-used silhouettes in the Underground's maw, the smell of too many children's bodies in a local
swimming pool, the aching chaos of a demolition site. The concept
of demolition exists at two separate, but undoubtedly related, levels
in Kossoff's work. Like Frank Auerbach, with whom he studied at St
Martin's School of Art, he regularly scrapes off his thickly layered
impasto into what he calls a 'grey mess' on the studio floor, destroying one picture to make way for another, in the hope that the desired
image will finally be caught in its coils. The sense of destruction is
rooted in his early memories, and in his feelings for London, whose
'endless streets and shuddering feel' (as Kossoff puts it) has provided
him with a subject for drawing and painting since he was a boy.

Kossoff's vanquished figures struggling through the city inevitably
recall the mood of Eliot's The Waste Land. And Eliot's feeling for London
also frequently foreshadows Auerbach's and Freud's evocations of its
bruised or seedy side – which in all three cases also reflect the intense
attachment that an adopted city inspires. Construction and demolition sites, great gashes of earth colours, have also held sway over
Auerbach's painterly imagination; and one commentator, the poet

Stephen Spender, has linked the subject to the artist's loss, at the age
of eight in Nazi Germany, of his whole childhood world. The other
urban scenes in Auerbach's work include Euston Steps, Primrose Hill,
and, more recently, a series of oil sketches of the approach to the
paint-encrusted studio where he has carried out his spectacular
impasto rituals since 1954. Freud's London is as specific and as precisely detailed as his portraits. 'My travelling', he has said, 'is
downwards, rather than outwards'; and the area he has explored most
thoroughly is Paddington, recording its broken-down interiors and
littered waste lots with meticulous emphasis.

A specific sense of place occurs more rarely in Bacon's work. Bacon
is so deeply rooted in London that he says he has never been able
to work as well elsewhere, but the whole Baconian atmosphere is that
of the anonymous room, a brightly-lit space that has been sealed off
from any identifiable 'outside'. Very occasionally, a particular area is
named, as in Isabel Rawsthorne Standing in a Street in Soho 1967; otherwise,
references to the city are extremely oblique. Soho itself has provided
the painters with a natural meeting ground, a fact that has been
eloquently recorded in Michael Andrews' picture of the Colony Room I
1962 (34), a well-known drinking club patronised by a very London
mix of artists and drifters. Among the regulars represented, one can
immediately spot Bacon, with his resilient back turned to the viewer,

and Freud, whose level stare gives the composition its focal point.

Other rallying points in Soho include the French pub (where the Free French drank together during the war) and the fish restaurant, Wheeler's, where Bacon entertains with legendary prodigality and verve. The London nightlife of private clubs which both Bacon and Freud have frequented bring to mind another artist to whom the night provided the real waking hours and who presides in certain ways over the School of London: Alberto Giacometti. Although Michael Andrews acknowledges that Giacometti had a strong influence over his earlier work and that his accomplishment was widely admired among English figurative artists, it was the Swiss sculptor's example – of stoic independence and total commitment to an exacting ideal – that made the most lasting impact. The disdain for art-world vogues and the apparent indifference to success that Giacometti embodies could not fail to impress a group of young artists whose belief in the human image had caused them to go directly counter to prevailing fashion, giving proof of what the art historian Andrew Forge has called a 'superb perseverance and a certain gritty satisfaction in hard times'.[5] And Frank Auerbach amplifies this when he says: 'One of the things that draws these painters together is the element of conscience, and [Mike Andrews'] extreme self-criticism does link him. I mean, all the painters in this group worry about pictures – we get them back and destroy them if we don't like them. And the element of inspiration – perhaps it's presumptuous to speak for other people – is as destructive as much as it's constructive and I think all of us tend to repaint them or destroy them. Lucian Freud had done one of his elaborate and hard-won heads and then chucked the whole thing away because it didn't seem to him to work … And Francis Bacon destroys constantly … So I think it is a question of spirit that [these painters] have in common, and a sense of isolation and certain degree of puritanical thoroughness.'[6]

Traces of Giacometti's effect on the School of London are still clearly discernible. Bacon got to know the Swiss artist well, and on one occasion spent an entire night in discussion with him. They respected each other's extreme individualism, and shared a stylish rejection of middle-class values. Like Giacometti, Bacon developed a highly personal code of behaviour while still a young, relatively unknown painter; and when fame and money came to him, he responded in a similar manner by not allowing them to alter the basic patterns of his life. Bacon's studio still retains something of the comfortless chaos of Giacometti's, but the most striking parallel to the sculptor's plaster-splattered cell is the shed-like structure in North London where Frank Auerbach has spent the past thirty-six years in intricate manipulations of vast quantities of oil paint. Over the decades of applying, scraping off, wiping, dripping and dropping the pigment, Auerbach has created for himself a cocoon of his colours into which only models and the odd friend are allowed. The artist maintains a strict working routine in this visually fascinating cell, rarely leaving it for life outside. He has been helped in this discipline, he says, by the fact that 'London takes no notice at all of its artists', adding, with some relish, 'I mean, there can be no nonsense here about artists sitting at café tables and having heated discussions.'[7]

A monastic sense of vocation dominates the London School studios. Extremely private spaces where nothing that does not serve the purposes of work is tolerated, they contain above all a mess of painter's materials and a few canvases in progress. Some reproductions or photos pinned to the wall and the occasional book, then nothing but the hours of doggedness and cunning to lure a new image into existence. Though not much in evidence in the studios, the literary and artistic resources on which these painters draw are prodigious. They are highly articulate and cultured men who read with an analytical urgency that allows them to gauge a book's qualities almost as swiftly as a painting's. Auerbach has given his view about the importance of reading very clearly: '… unless one has the sort of speculative intelligence that makes one invent oneself, which is really what reading a book does, I don't think one can last as a painter. Everybody I know, who paints, Lucian Freud or Leon Kossoff, or anybody who seems to me to have shown some sort of sustained level of artistic invention, has read books.'[8] To talk about Greek tragedy with Bacon or German poetry with Freud is a privilege, because, as painters, they come at the subject from a fresh, unexpected angle, and with an insight that stems perhaps from the way they ransack literature for what it might bring to their art.

They are no less compelling, of course, when they talk about painting. Although the range of their admirations is relatively wide, they look above all towards the great European masters. Bacon's obsession with Velázquez's Portrait of Pope Innocent X is the most obvious example; but his indirect borrowings and references range from Egyptian art to photography, with Michelangelo, Degas and Van Gogh being particularly important sources, while Picasso has perhaps had the most pervasive, formal influence over him.[9] If the other artists do not follow the same 'long call from antiquity' that Bacon has mentioned in his talks with David Sylvester, they all refer to the past, sometimes to the point of making variations on old master themes – a practice that, Picasso apart, has virtually fallen into disuse in our century. Freud's natural adherence to the Northern European tradition seems evident from the enamelled precision of the paintings he was executing at the time of his portrait of Bacon (1952). But he has also paid a manifest tribute to Watteau, the master of flesh and silk, by basing the composition of his Large Interior, W.11 (after Watteau) 1981-3 on the pyramid of figures in Pierrot Content. Auerbach, who is an assiduous visitor to London's National Gallery ('it would be ludicrous to imagine that paintings come out of thin air', he says), has rendered the same kind of homage to Rembrandt, while Kossoff has reworked themes by Rubens and Poussin. In this sense, they have engaged like no other artists of their generation with the living tradition of the European old masters.

It is worth reflecting on the singular isolation that the London painters seem less to have endured than to have encouraged. As they came increasingly into their own in the two decades following the Second World War, it would have been borne in on them that New York had replaced Paris as the centre of stylistic invention, and that even the new generation of French painters were looking more towards America than to their own past. Many of the most potent influences of the period – from international abstraction to the fascination with tribal art and the consequences of Duchamp – made little apparent impression on their development. The latest issue of *Cahiers d'Art*, the aura surrounding Picasso or the exploits of Balthus recounted in the cafés of Saint-Germain-des-Prés carried altogether more weight in that particular London ambience than any report from downtown lofts and the Cedar Tavern. The anecdote recounted by John Russell about Lucian Freud's being so energetically eager to explore Paris as a young man that his bicycle broke under him exemplifies that attraction.

The bond between the London painters – which they themselves acknowledge in part and partly disavow – was originally forged in the 1950s, when the peculiarity of pursuing figurative images in a time dominated by the theory and practice of abstraction made them natural allies. The Giacometti-like steadfastness and 'gritty satisfaction in hard times' that enabled them to swim so directly against the tide of fashion found an unusual champion in the person of Helen Lessore, a painter who turned by force of circumstances to running the Beaux Arts Gallery for some fourteen years. She recognised and encouraged the talent of Bacon, Freud, Auerbach, Andrews and Kossoff, and she took all but one of them in hand (Freud was scheduled to have a show, but signed up with another gallery before it took place). With our thirty years' hindsight, the Beaux Arts' programme sounds less like the daring, precarious venture it was than a rollcall of honour, with an exhibition of Michael Andrews in 1952, of Francis Bacon in 1953, of Frank Auerbach in 1956, of Leon Kossoff in 1957 – and several more of these and other gifted artists before the gallery folded in 1965.

It was typical of that period that an admirer of any of these artists would soon be introduced to the others. When I was editing the undergraduate magazine *Cambridge Opinion* in 1963, an initial meeting with Francis Bacon quickly led to introductions to Lucian Freud and Frank Auerbach. All three artists in fact contributed statements or interviews to an issue of that magazine entitled 'Modern Art in Britain', which began to make apparent the similarities of their attitudes and aims.[10] After the Beaux Arts Gallery had closed down, several of the artists went on to exhibit regularly at Marlborough Fine Art (which represents Bacon and Auerbach to this day), and from recent interviews it is clear that they retain the greatest admiration for each other's achievements.

The most retiring of a reclusive group (a 'herd of loners', to use Kitaj's expression), Michael Andrews has talked very little about his work, and indeed his delicate, ambiguous imagery skilfully deflects most attempts at interpretation. In many senses, Andrews is the most 'English' of the London artists. Irony, an eccentric humour, a Romantic identification with landscape and a distaste for obvious effect inform his all too rarely seen paintings. His compositions are never more elusive than when they seem most close to a naturalistic representation of their subject. Andrews maintains a hair's-breadth between the reality and its translation into acrylic or watercolour. Within that narrow, enigmatic area, he captures appearances accurately while subjecting them to a kind of astonished scrutiny – as if to recall the mystery inherent in the very act of seeing.

Andrews' use of paint is thin and sparing, as far removed from Auerbach's luscious, swirling impasto as could be imagined. Where they come together – indeed, where all these London painters meet – is in the dislocation of appearance: reflective and controlled in Andrews, impassioned and instinctive in Auerbach. It is as if one went from Stendhal, where one is not conscious of the medium, to Joyce, where the experiment, the will to 'make it new', is apparent at every turn. In early Auerbach, the image was impounded in relief-deep pigment, surfacing at certain moments, then merging back into its matrix. It has worked its way slowly up to the surface, and now performs its transformations within the same plane. The look of suddenness, of having been just splashed down, from which his images derive their potent spontaneity, comes in a moment of grace after months of laborious building up and scraping off. The essential

Lucian Freud *Frank Auerbach* 1975-6

activity takes place so much in the paint itself that, in Auerbach's case, words prove especially inadequate; and the most acute commentator of his work remains the artist himself.[11]

For Francis Bacon, the same claim might be made, since his conversation often amplifies the impact of his imagery and takes his viewers closer to his tragic, but extraordinarily vitalising, attitude to life. The most Nietzschean of painters, Bacon has furiously stripped existence of any ultimate meaning and yet infused it with a contorted, purely man-made grandeur.

Paradoxically, he might be seen as the great 'religious' painter of the century, since his work has – as no one else's – always addressed the fundamental issues in the sheerest and most searching manner. In pictorial terms, he is also profoundly resourceful, turning the smallest detail to expressive advantage, such as the repetition of certain objects or devices which, as in some highly symbolic theatre, take on a ritualistic significance. The oldest and best known of these artists, Bacon has been a model of intellectual freedom and stylistic audacity to the whole School of London.

Existential anguish lies embedded in the very grain of Leon Kossoff's paint. His bowed figures are crushed by its pervasive presence – which, one senses, might be a haunting memory of ignominy and pain, a fear of suffering which has become a state of suffering. Kossoff's parents were Russian Jews, and in his frequent portraits of them and other family members, a whole heritage of oppression is voiced. At first sight, the sense of pathos is overpowering, but it rests on a rockbed of endurance. Gnarled and lacerated, Kossoff's figures are nevertheless survivors. Occasionally, what the artist has called the 'pain of the present' appears to lighten. An element of hope, however tremulous, rises in the little sprigs of flesh that people the *Children's Swimming Pool* series as well as in Kossoff's magnificent reworkings of great classical compositions, such as Poussin's *Cephalus and Aurora* or Rubens' *Minerva Protects Pax from Mars*. Once the first wave of Kossoff's melancholy has been absorbed, the eye becomes more conscious of the extraordinary intricacy and subtlety of his paint. Although the artist's London roots are eloquently recorded throughout his work, its atmosphere remains predominantly Central European or Slav, closer to the dark foreboding of his teacher, David Bomberg, or to Soutine's bewildered pathos than to any inherently English model.

Where Andrews and Bacon make frequent sophisticated use of photographs in the development of their imagery, Auerbach, Kossoff and Freud all prefer to work from a model. For Freud, this is an article of faith: 'I am never inhibited by working from life', he says. 'On the contrary, I feel more free; and I can take liberties which the tyranny of memory would not allow.'[12] Freud is arguably the most penetrating portraitist at work today. He takes possession of his sitters; and when they are returned in paint, they are in every sense his creation. Over the burly professional men as much as over the supine nudes, one senses an extraordinary will to define human presence enduringly. 'I want paint to *work as flesh* ...', Freud has explained. 'I know my idea of portraiture came from dissatisfaction with portraits that resembled people. I would wish my portraits to be of the people,

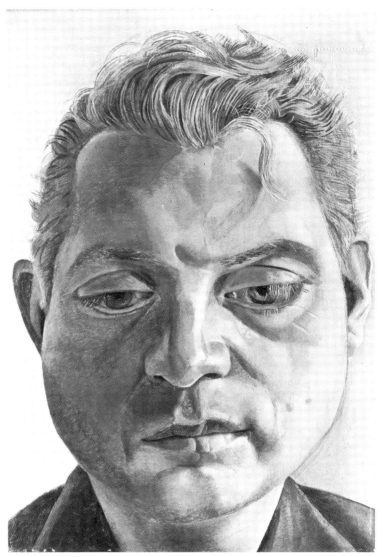

Lucian Freud *Francis Bacon* 1952

not *like* them. Not having the look of the sitter, *being* them ... As far as I am concerned the paint *is* the person.'[13] In the absoluteness of this equation, Freud has restored portraiture to a level where the image becomes the test and the mirror of a dual truth.

If all the factors that have brought about the School of London phenomenon could be assembled, chance (or, some might say, history) would loom large among them. Three out of the five artists discussed were born to parents brought up in German or Russian traditions; and another, Francis Bacon, was marked forever by an upbringing in the very different milieu of Ireland. So to say that they automatically reach beyond a specifically British heritage is less an opinion than a statement of fact. It may be that their instinctive awareness of the larger European tradition (further developed in Auerbach and Kossoff by their teacher, Bomberg, and in Bacon by his early sojourns in Berlin and Paris) resulted in their being more keenly attuned to what happened on the Continent than to the later developments of modernism in America. The group's immediate forebears, as I have pointed out, are predominantly European, with Matisse, Picasso, Giacometti and Balthus being the most obvious among them. And in many ways, they have become the natural heirs to those artists, for whom it would be difficult to find any such direct successors in France. In this sense, the London painters have not only been formed by European tradition; they are the manifest continuation of it.

Notes

1. Organised by the British Council, the exhibition went to Oslo, the Louisiana Museum in Denmark, to Venice and Düsseldorf. The present essay is an enlarged and revised version of the preface that I wrote for the catalogue of the exhibition.
2. Preface to *The Human Clay*, Arts Council of Great Britain exhibition catalogue 1976. Other essays worth consulting include Timothy Hyman's introduction to *Narrative Paintings*, an exhibition at Arnolfini, Bristol 1979; Lawrence Gowing's preface to *Eight Figurative Painters*, at the Yale Center for British Art, New Haven 1981; Richard Morphet's text in *The Hard-Won Image*, Tate Gallery, London 1984; and Dawn Ades' two contributions to *British Art in the 20th Century*, Royal Academy, London 1987.
3. I am indebted to Alice Bellony-Rewald for suggesting the comparison with the Impressionists.
4. Interview in *Art International*, Autumn 1987, pp.22-9.
5. Andrew Forge, in his preface to *Eight Figurative Painters*, *op. cit.* n.2, p.6.
6. *op. cit.* n.4.
7. *op. cit.* n.4.
8. Catherine Lampert, 'A Conversation with Frank Auerbach', in *Frank Auerbach*, Arts Council of Great Britain exhibition catalogue, London 1978, p.21.
9. I have given a more complete account of Bacon's sources in 'Francis Bacon: The Anatomy of Enigma', *Art International*, September-November 1984.
10. 'Modern Art in Britain', *Cambridge Opinion*, no.37, Cambridge 1964.
11. See, for example, not only the interview with the artist published in this issue but also in Catherine Lampert's 'A Conversation with Frank Auerbach', *op. cit.* n.8, and Auerbach's own writings listed in *Frank Auerbach, Recent Work*, Marlborough Fine Art exhibition catalogue, London 1983.
12. Quoted by John Russell in his preface to *Lucian Freud*, Hayward Gallery, London, Arts Council of Great Britain exhibition catalogue 1974, p.5.
13. Quoted by Lawrence Gowing in *Lucian Freud*, London 1982, pp.190-1.

WALTER RICHARD SICKERT

1920	Christine died
1924	Elected ARA. Adopted name Richard Sickert
1926	Married Thérèse Lessore. Taught at Royal Academy Schools
1927	Settled in Islington
1934	Settled at St Peter's-in-Thanet near Margate. Taught at Thanet School of Art. Elected RA
1935	Resigned from Royal Academy in support of Epstein's British Medical Association sculpture
1938	Moved to Bathampton near Bath
1942	Died on 22 January

Selected solo exhibitions

1900	Durand-Ruel, Paris
1904	Bernheim-Jeune Gallery, Paris
1907,1909	Bernheim-Jeune Gallery, Paris
1911,12, 14,16	Carfax Gallery, London
1926,28,30	Savile Gallery, London
1929	Retrospective exhibition, Leicester Galleries, London
1930	Galerie Cardo, Paris
1931	English Echoes, Leicester Galleries, London
1932,33,35	Beaux Arts Gallery
1933	Thomas Agnew & Sons, London
1938	The Arts Club, Chicago and Carnegie Institute, Pittsburgh
1941	Retrospective exhibition, National Gallery, London
1942	Retrospective exhibition, Temple Newsam House, Leeds
1949	Arts Council of Great Britain, London
1950	Museum of Art, Hove
1951	Roland, Browse and Delbanco, London
1953	Arts Council of Great Britain, Edinburgh
1957	Graves Art Gallery, Sheffield
1960	Thomas Agnew & Sons. Centenary loan exhibition, Tate Gallery, London and tour (Arts Council of Great Britain touring exhibition)
1962	Royal Pavilion, Brighton
1964	Arts Council of Great Britain, Midlands touring exhibition
1967	Hirschl & Adler Galleries, New York
1968	Art Gallery of South Australia, Adelaide
1970	Islington Town Hall, Islington Public Libraries collection
1977-78	Ferens Art Gallery, Hull and tour (Arts Council of Great Britain touring exhibition)
1981	Late Sickert, Hayward Gallery, London and tour (Arts Council of Great Britain touring exhibition)
1989	Tate Gallery, Liverpool

Extensively represented in group exhibitions

1860	Born in Munich
1868	Moved to England
c.1879-81	Toured the provinces as an actor
1881	Studied briefly at the Slade School of Fine Art. Became apprenticed to Whistler
1883	First meeting with Degas
1885	Married Ellen Cobden
1887-89	Concentrated on painting London's music halls
1888	Joined the New English Art Club
1890-95	Contributed illustrations, portraits and caricatures to various journals
1895	First visit to Venice
1898-1905	Moved to Dieppe and made visits to Venice in 1900, 1901 and 1903-04
1899	Divorced from Ellen
1905	Returned to London. Summer in Dieppe
1906	Rejoined the New English Art Club
1907	Fitzroy Street Group began informally
1908-18	Teaching at Westminster Technical Institute
1911	Married Christine Angus
1911-13	Camden Town Group formed
1916-19	Spent time in Bath
1919	Moved to Envermeu near Dieppe

I
Walter Richard Sickert
Mamma Mia Poveretta
c. 1903-4

3
Walter Richard Sickert
Hubby and Marie
c. 1912

2
Walter Richard Sickert
Le Lit de Cuivre
c. 1906

4
Walter Richard Sickert
La Scierie de Torqueville
1913

5
Walter Richard Sickert
Interior with Nude
1914

6
Walter Richard Sickert
Victor Lecour
1922-4

8
Walter Richard Sickert
High Steppers
c.1938-9

9
Walter Richard Sickert
Alexander Gavin Henderson, 2nd Lord Faringdon

10

Walter Richard Sickert
The Temple Bar
c.1941

DAVID BOMBERG

1890	Born in Birmingham
1895	Moved to Whitechapel, London
c.1906-07	Studied with Walter Bayes at the City and Guilds evening classes. Apprentice lithographer in Islington
1908-10	Central School of Arts and Crafts, evening classes in book production and lithography with W. R. Lethaby. Attended Sickert's evening classes at the Westminster Technical School
1911-14	Slade School of Art. Taught by Fred Brown and Henry Tonks. Founder-member of the London Group. Moved into artists' commune in Ormonde Terrace
1915	Enlisted in the Royal Engineers and subsequently transferred to the 18th King's Royal Rifles
1916	Married Alice Hayes. Active service in France
1917	Canadian War Memorials Fund commission to paint *Sappers at Work*
1919	Completed second accepted version of *Sappers at Work*
1920-22	Lived in Alton, Hampshire
1923	Met Lilian Mendelson (née Holt). Left for Palestine funded by the Keren Hayesod (Palestine Foundation Fund). Settled in Jerusalem
1927	Returned to England
1929	First trip to Spain. Worked in Toledo
1933	Joined Communist Party and visited Moscow. Resigned on return
1934	Returned to Spain. Worked in Cuenca and then Ronda, Andalucia
1935	Moved to Linares in Asturian Mountains above valley of La Hermida. Returned to London
1941	Married Lilian Mendelson
1942	Commissioned by War Artists' Advisory Committee to paint underground bomb store at RAF Fauld, Tutbury, near Burton-on-Trent
1944	Part-time teaching at Hammersmith, Battersea and Clapham. Painted and drew bomb-damaged London. Visited North Wales
1945-49	Teaching at Bartlett School of Architecture, London
1945-53	Teaching at the Borough Polytechnic, London
1946	Summer painting expedition to North Devon
1947	Summer painting expedition to Cornwall
1948	Summer painting expedition to Cyprus
1953	The Borough Bottega formed
1954-57	Moved to Ronda, Andalucia. Attempted to found a School of Painting at the Villa Paz
1955-57	Lived at La Casa de la Virgen de la Cabeza near Ronda
1957	Resigned from the London Group. Became seriously ill and died 19 August

Selected solo exhibitions

1914	Chenil Gallery, London
1919	Exhibition of drawings, Adelphi Gallery, London
1923	Heal's Mansard Gallery, London
1928	*Paintings of Palestine and Petra*, Leicester Galleries, London
1929	One-man exhibition of Palestine and Petra paintings, Ruskin Gallery, Birmingham
1932	*Sixty Imaginative Compositions, Spanish and Scottish Landscapes and Other Work*, Bloomsbury Gallery, London
1936	*Recent Paintings of Spain*, Cooling Galleries, London
1937	Foyle Art Gallery, London with Margarete Hamerschlag and Horace Brodzky
1943	*Imaginative Compositions*, Leger Gallery, London
1954	Heffer Gallery, Cambridge (with a Borough Bottega show)
1958	*David Bomberg 1890-1957, An Exhibition of Paintings and Drawings*, Arts Council Gallery, London
1960	Herbert Art Gallery, Coventry
1961	Hope Hall, Liverpool
1964	Marlborough Fine Art, London
1967	*David Bomberg 1890-1957*, Tate Gallery, London and Arts Council of Great Britain tour
1971	Reading Art Gallery with Lilian Holt
1973	Fischer Fine Art, London
1979	*David Bomberg: The Later Years*, Whitechapel Art Gallery, London
1981	*Works from the collection of Lilian Bomberg*, Anthony d'Offay Gallery, London
1983	*David Bomberg in Palestine 1923-1927*, The Israel Museum, Jerusalem
1984	*David Bomberg in the Holy Land 1923-1927*, Ben Uri Gallery, London
1985	*David Bomberg: A Tribute to Lilian Bomberg*, Fischer Fine Art, London
1986	L. A. Louver Gallery, Venice, California. Rex Irwin Gallery, Woollahra, Australia.
1988	Tate Gallery, London and tour. Fischer Fine Art, London

Selected group exhibitions

1913	*The Camden Town Group and Others*, 'Cubist Room', Brighton Art Galleries
1914	First London Group exhibition, London. *Twentieth Century Art: A Review of Modern Movements*, Whitechapel Art Gallery, London
1915	'Invited to Show' section, first Vorticist exhibition, Doré Galleries, London
1919	London Group exhibition, London
1920	New English Art Club exhibitions, London. London Group exhibition
1922	London Group exhibition
1923	New English Art Club
1926	New English Art Club
1927	*Jewish Art and Antiquities*, Whitechapel Art Gallery, London
1928	London Group retrospective exhibition 1914-1928
1929	*Contemporary British Art*, Whitechapel Art Gallery, London
1931-35	National Society annual exhibitions
1932	Contemporary British art exhibition, Kunstverein, Hamburg
1936	*Contemporary British Painting*, British Council exhibition, National Gallery of Canada, Ottawa
1937	London Group exhibition
1938	National Society exhibition
1939	*Mural Painting in Great Britain 1919-1939*, Tate Gallery, London London Group exhibition
1943,44, 46-49,51,52	London Group exhibitions
1948	Second exhibition of the Borough Group, Archer Gallery, London
1949	Third exhibition of the Borough Group, Arcade Gallery, London
1953	*Drawings and Paintings by The Borough Bottega and L. Marr and D. Scott*, Berkeley Galleries, London
1954	Borough Bottega exhibition, Black Hall, Oxford. London Group exhibition
1955,56	London Group exhibition
1987	*British Art in the 20th Century: The Modern Movement*, Royal Academy of Arts, London

11
David Bomberg
Mount Zion with the Church of the Dormition : Moonlight
1923

12
David Bomberg
Jerusalem, Looking to Mount Scopus
1925

13
David Bomberg
Toledo and River Tajo
1929

14
David Bomberg
Ronda : In the Gorge of the Tajo
1935

15
David Bomberg
Sunrise in the Mountains, Picos de Asturias
1935

17
David Bomberg
Evening in the City of London
1944

18
David Bomberg
Castle Ruins, St Hilarion, Cyprus
1948

STANLEY SPENCER

1891	Born in Cookham-on-Thames, Berkshire
1908-12	Studied at the Slade School of Fine Art under Henry Tonks
1910	Awarded a scholarship
1915-18	Enlisted in the Royal Army Medical Corps and posted to the Beaufort War Hospital, Bristol
1916	Sent to Macedonia and served with 68th, 66th and 143rd Field Ambulances
1917	Volunteered and joined 7th battalion, Royal Berkshires. Commissioned to paint an official war painting before return to England in December 1918
1919	Became member of the New English Art Club. Worked in Cookham
1920	Stayed at Durweston in Dorset with Henry Lamb
1922	Visit to Yugoslavia with the Carlines. Moved to Hampstead
1923	Enrolled for spring term at the Slade. Stayed with Henry Lamb in Dorset
1925	Married Anne Hilda Carline
1927	Moved to Burghclere to decorate the Memorial Chapel built by Mr and Mrs J.L.Behrend
1932	Completed the Memorial Chapel and returned to Cookham. Elected ARA. Dudley Tooth became Spencer's sole agent
1935	Resigned from Royal Academy after rejection of *Lovers and St Francis and the Birds* by the hanging committee
1937	Divorced by Hilda. Married Patricia Preece. Visits to St Ives and Southwold

1940	Commissioned to paint pictures of shipyards by the War Artists' Advisory Committee and made the first of several visits to Lithgow's Yard, Port Glasgow
1942-44	Returned to Cookham and continued to work on the *Shipbuilders* and made visits to Port Glasgow
1947	Burghclere Chapel presented to the National Trust
1950	Rejoined the Royal Academy and elected RA
1954	Visited China as part of a cultural delegation
1958	Knighted
1959	Died at the Canadian War Memorial Hospital, Cliveden

Selected solo exhibitions

1927	Goupil Gallery, London
1932,36,50	Arthur Tooth & Sons
1939	J.Leger and Son, London
1942	Leicester Galleries, London
1947	Retrospective exhibition, Temple Newsam House, Leeds
1954	*Drawings by Stanley Spencer*, Arts Council of Great Britain
1955	Retrospective exhibition, Tate Gallery, London
1961	Worthing Art Gallery, Worthing
1962-	King's Hall, Cookham-on-Thames, Stanley Spencer Gallery opened
1963	City Museum and Art Gallery, Plymouth
1975	*Stanley Spencer, War Artist on Clydeside 1940-45*, Scottish Arts Council, Third Eye Centre, Glasgow
1976-77	Arts Council of Great Britain retrospective exhibition, Brighton Art Gallery and tour
1979	*Stanley Spencer in the Shipyard*, Imperial War Museum and the Science Museum, London
1980	Retrospective exhibition, Royal Academy of Arts, London

Selected group exhibitions

1912	*Second Post-Impressionist Exhibition*, Grafton Galleries, London. New English Art Club, London
1913	*Contemporary Art Society*, Goupil Gallery, London
1914	*Twentieth Century Art*, Whitechapel Art Gallery, London
1919-20	*The Imperial War Museum, The Nation's War Paintings*, Royal Academy of Arts, London
1919-27	New English Art Club exhibitions
1923	*Contemporary Art Society*, Grosvenor House, London
1924	*British Empire Exhibition*, Wembley
1929	*Contemporary British Art*, Whitechapel Art Gallery, London
1932	*Venice Biennale*
1933	*Sarah Tubb* exhibited, Carnegie Institute, Pittsburgh
1938	*Venice Biennale*
1946	*Exposition de Peintures Modernes*, UNESCO, Musée d'Art Moderne, Paris
1948	*Contemporary Painting in Britain*, British Council exhibition, Palais des Beaux-Arts, Brussels
1953	*Paintings and Drawings from the Sir Edward Marsh Collection*, Arts Council of Great Britain
1961	*Three Masters of Modern British Painting (Ivon Hitchens, Stanley Spencer, Graham Sutherland)*, Arts Council of Great Britain, Second Series, touring exhibition
1966	*British Painting and Sculpture: 1900-1950*, Arthur Tooth & Sons, London
1968-69	*Royal Academy of Arts Bicentenary Exhibition. 1768-1968*, Royal Academy of Arts, London
1970	*A Decade 1920-30*, Arts Council of Great Britain
1971	*The Slade 1871-1971*, Royal Academy of Arts, London
1972	*A Decade 1940-49*, Arts Council of Great Britain
1976	*An Honest Patron (Sir Edward Marsh)*, Bluecoat Gallery, Liverpool
1977	*British Painting 1952-77*, Royal Academy of Arts, London
1977-78	*The Bible in British Art*, Victoria and Albert Museum, London
1979-80	*The Thirties*, Hayward Gallery, London
1980	*Pictures for an Exhibition*, Whitechapel Art Gallery, London
1987	*British Art in the 20th Century: The Modern Movement*, Royal Academy of Arts, London

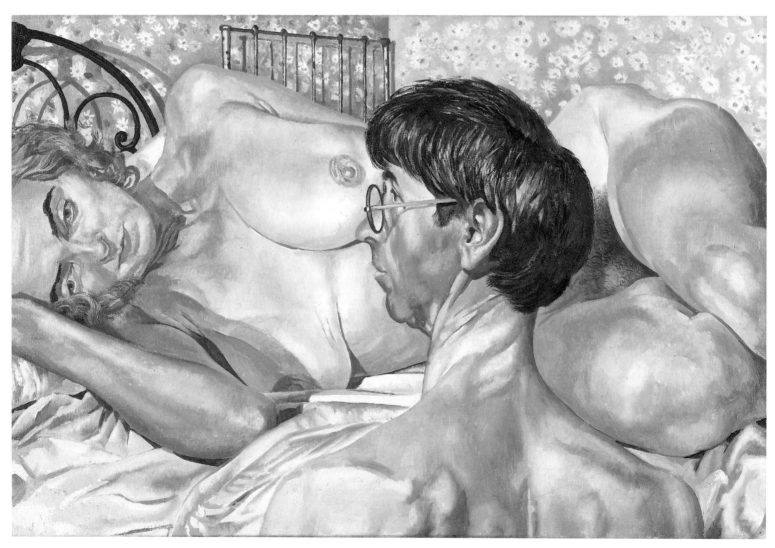

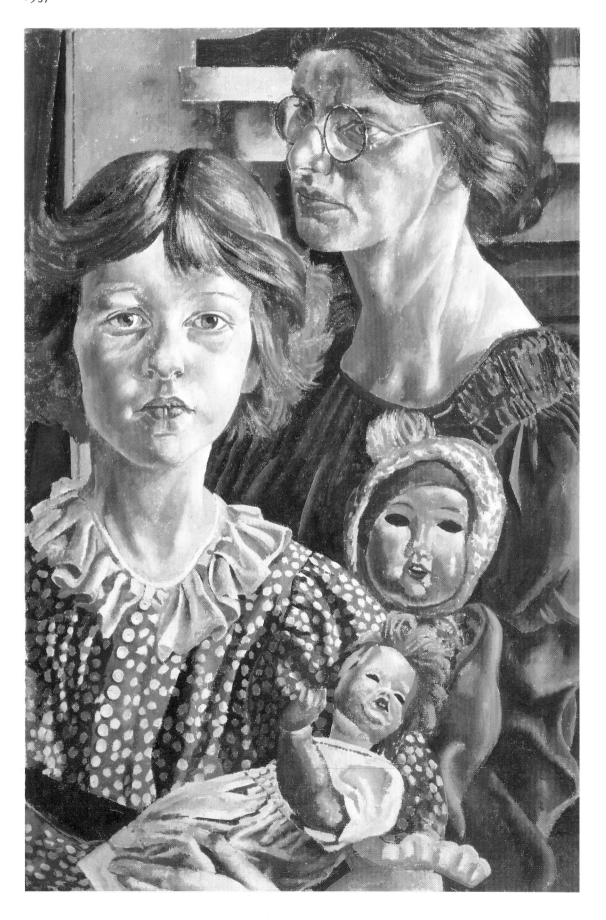

23
Stanley Spencer
The Vale of Health, Hampstead
1939

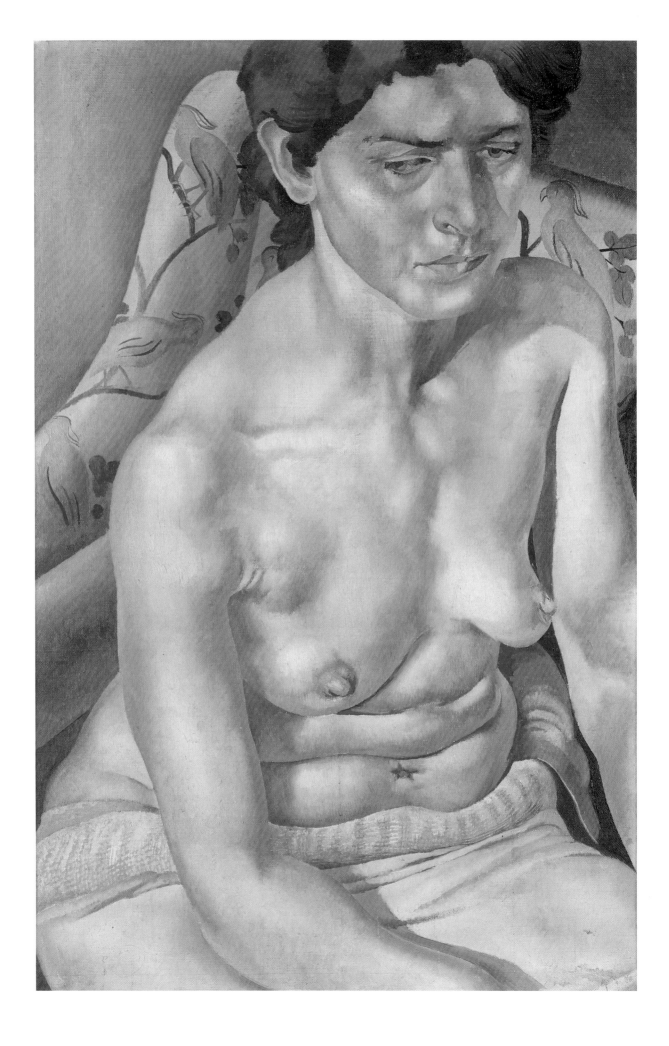

25
Stanley Spencer
The Psychiatrist
1945

26 OPPOSITE
Stanley Spencer
Portrait of Dame Mary Cartwright, FRS, ScD
1958

WILLIAM COLDSTREAM

1908	Born in Belford, Northumberland
1926-29	Studied at the Slade School of Fine Art, London
1929	Exhibited with the New English Art Club and the London Group
1934	Elected to the London Group. Worked with the GPO Film Unit under John Grierson
1935	Directed short colour film, *The King's Stamp*. Worked on the film *Coal Face* with W. H. Auden
1937	Took up full-time painting again. Encouraged by Sir Kenneth Clark
1938	Visited Bolton with Graham Bell at the suggestion of Tom Harrison of Mass Observation. With Claude Rogers and Victor Pasmore founded the Euston Road School
1943-45	Official War Artist in Middle East and Italy
1945	Taught at Camberwell School of Arts and Crafts
1948-63	Trustee of the National Gallery. Trustee of the Tate Gallery
1949-75	Slade Professor of Fine Art at University College, London
1952	Awarded CBE
1953-62	Chairman of the Art Panel of the Arts Council of Great Britain
1956	Knighted
1958-71	Chairman of the National Advisory Council on Art Education
1962-70	Vice-chairman of the Arts Council of Great Britain
1964-71	Chairman of the British Film Institute
1987	Died February

Selected solo exhibitions

1933	London Artists Association exhibition with H. E. Du Plessis, Cooling Galleries, London
1962	Retrospective exhibition, South London Art Gallery and Arts Council tour
1976	Anthony d'Offay Gallery, London
1984	Anthony d'Offay Gallery, London

Selected group exhibitions

1939	British *Art Since Whistler*, National Gallery, London
1946	*Exposition de Peintures Modernes*, UNESCO, Musée d'Art Moderne, Paris
1964	*Painting and Sculpture of a Decade 1954-64*, Tate Gallery, London
1971	*The Slade 1871-1971*, Royal Academy of Arts, London
1976	*The Human Clay*, Hayward Gallery, London and tour (Arts Council of Great Britain touring exhibition)
1977	*British Painting 1952-77*, Royal Academy of Arts, London
1984	*The Hard-Won Image*, Tate Gallery, London
1987	*British Art in the 20th Century: The Modern Movement*, Royal Academy of Arts, London

William Coldstream
Portrait of Stephen Spender
1937

28
William Coldstream
Cripplegate
c. 1946 - 7

29

William Coldstream

Reclining Nude

1953-4

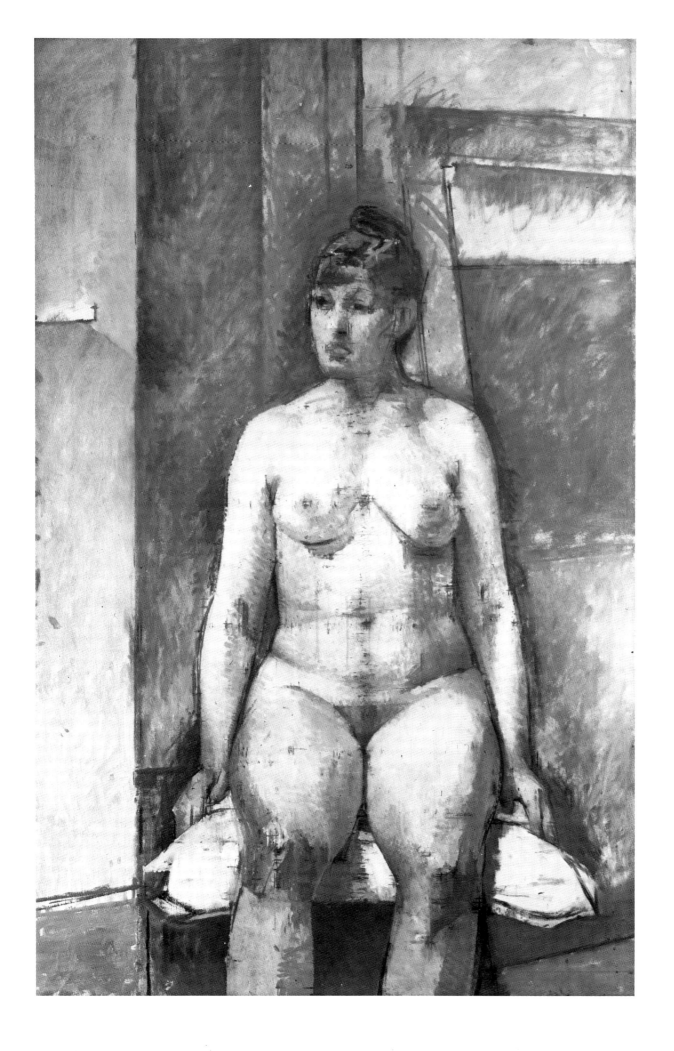

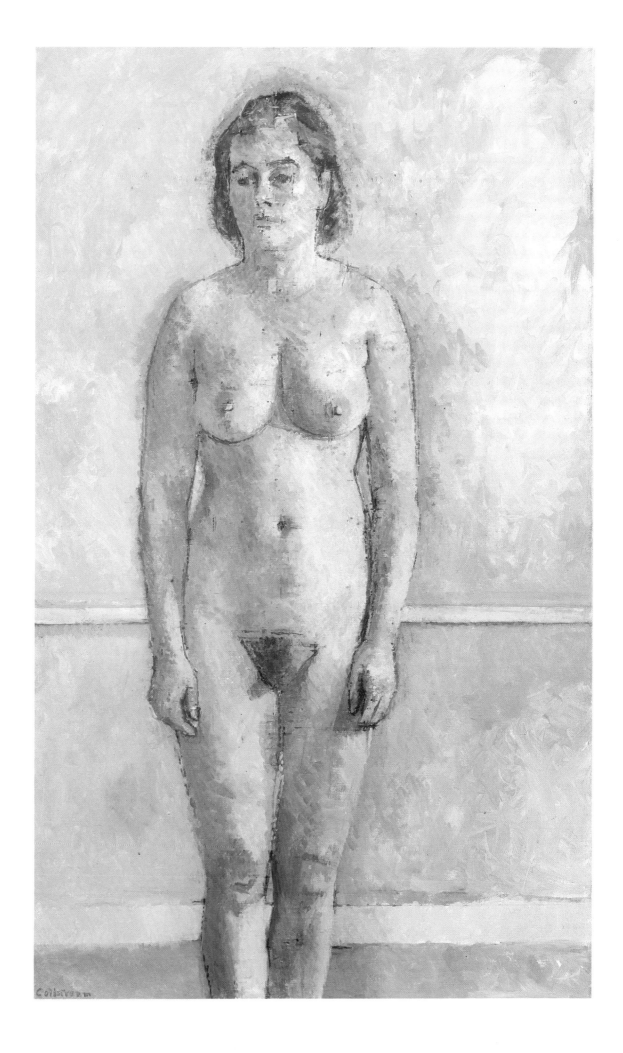

30 OPPOSITE
William Coldstream
Seated Nude
1960

31 RIGHT
William Coldstream
Standing Nude
1977-8

William Coldstream
Westminster VI
1978

MICHAEL ANDREWS

1928	Born in Norwich
1945-53	Studied at the Slade School of Fine Art
1953	Rome Scholarship in Painting
1958-59	Lived at the Digswell Arts Trust
1959-66	Taught at Norwich School of Art, the Slade School of Fine Art and Chelsea School of Art
1961	Received Gulbenkian Purchase Award
1973	Invited to use the Visitor's Studio at the Royal College of Art for 6 months
1977	Moved from London back to Norfolk
1983	Visited Ayers Rock in Australia

Lives and works in Norfolk

Selected solo exhibitions

1958,63	Beaux Arts Gallery, London
1974	Anthony d'Offay Gallery, London
1978	*Paintings 1977-78*, Anthony d'Offay Gallery, London
1980-81	Retrospective exhibition, Hayward Gallery, London and tour
1986	*Rock of Ages Cleft for Me*, Anthony d'Offay Gallery, London

Selected group exhibitions

1952	*Four Young Artists*, Beaux Arts Gallery, London. *Young Painters*, Institute of Contemporary Arts, London
1953	*Drawings for Pictures*, Arts Council of Great Britain
1955	*8 Painters*, Institute of Contemporary Arts, London
	6 Young Painters, Arts Council of Great Britain, London
1960-61	*Modern British Portraits*, The Arts Council Gallery, Cambridge and tour
1962	*British Self Portraits from Sickert to the Present Day*, Arts Council of Great Britain, London
1964	*Painting and Sculpture of a Decade 1954-64*, Tate Gallery, London. *British Painting in the '60s*, Whitechapel Art Gallery, London
1964-65	*Pittsburgh International 1964*, Carnegie Institute, Pittsburgh
1966	*Survey 66 : Figurative Art*, Camden Arts Centre, London
1967	*Drawing Towards Painting 2*, Arts Council of Great Britain. *English Painting 1951-1967*, Norwich Castle Museum, Norwich
1968	*Helen Lessore and the Beaux Arts Gallery*, Marlborough Fine Art, London
1971	*The Slade 1871-1971*, Royal Academy of Arts, London
1972	*Tercera Bienal de Arte Coltejar*, Medellin, Colombia
1973	*Critic's Choice*, selected by Michael Shepherd, Arthur Tooth & Sons, London
1974	*Contemporary British Painting and Sculpture*, Lefevre Gallery, London
1977	*Real Life : Peter Moores Liverpool Project*, Walker Art Gallery, Liverpool. *British Painting 1952-1977*, Royal Academy of Arts, London
1979-80	*Narrative Painting*, Institute of Contemporary Arts, London and tour. *The British Art Show*, Mappin Art Gallery, Sheffield and tour (Arts Council of Great Britain touring exhibition)
1981-82	*Eight Figurative Painters*, Yale Center for British Art, New Haven, Connecticut
1982	*British Drawings and Watercolours*, British Council tour, People's Republic of China
1983	*As of Now : Peter Moores Liverpool Project*, The Walker Art Gallery, Liverpool
1984	*The Hard-Won Image*, Tate Gallery, London. *Modern Masters from the Thyssen-Bornemisza Collection*, Royal Academy of Arts, London
1984-85	*The Proper Study : Contemporary Figurative Paintings from Britain*, British Council tour, New Delhi and Bombay
1985	*A Singular Vision*, Royal Albert Memorial Museum and Art Gallery, Exeter and tour
1986	*Gallery Artists*, Anthony d'Offay Gallery, London. *Robin Campbell Commemorative Exhibition*, Arts Council of Great Britain, Smiths Galleries, London
1986-87	*Looking into Paintings*, Arts Council of Great Britain, Castle Museum, Nottingham and tour
1987	*British Art in the 20th Century : The Modern Movement*, Royal Academy of Arts, London
1987-88	*A School of London : Six Figurative Painters*, British Council tour, Kunstnernes Hus, Oslo

33 ABOVE
Michael Andrews
The Family in the Garden
1960-2

34 RIGHT
Michael Andrews
The Colony Room I
1962

THE SHIP ENGULFED

37
Michael Andrews
Self-Portrait
1988

FRANK AUERBACH

1931   Born in Berlin
1939   Arrived in London
1948-52   Studied at St Martin's School of Art, London
1952-55   Studied at the Royal College of Art, London

Lives and works in London

Selected solo exhibitions

1959,60,61,   Beaux Arts Gallery, London
62,63
1965,67,71,   Marlborough Fine Art, London
72,74,83,87
1969   Marlborough-Gerson Gallery, New York
1973   University of Essex, Colchester
1975   Municipal Art Gallery, Dublin
1976   Marlborough Galerie, Zurich
1978   Anthony d'Offay Gallery, London. Retrospective exhibition,
               Hayward Gallery, London
1979   Bernard Jacobson, New York
1982   Marlborough Galley Inc., New York
1983   Anne Berthoud Gallery, London
1986   *Venice Biennale*, British Pavilion
1987   Folkwang Museum, Essen and Centro de Arte Reina Sofia, Madrid

Selected group exhibitions

1958   *Critic's Choice* (David Sylvester), Tooth & Sons, London
1964   *British Painting in the Sixties*, organised by the Contemporary Art Society,
           Tate Gallery, London and Whitechapel Art Gallery, London.
           54-64 Painting and Sculpture of a Decade, Tate Gallery, London
1968   *Helen Lessore and the Beaux Arts Gallery*, Marlborough Fine Art, London
1976   *Drawings of People*, Serpentine Gallery, London and tour (Arts Council
           of Great Britain touring exhibition). *The Human Clay*, Hayward
           Gallery, London and tour (Arts Council of Great Britain touring
           exhibition)
1977   *British Painting 1952-77*, Royal Academy of Arts, London
1977-78   *Francis Bacon and Frank Auerbach Recent Paintings*, Marlborough Fine Art,
           London
1977,80   *Hayward Annual*, Hayward Gallery, London
1981-82   *Eight Figurative Artists*, Yale Center for British Art, New Haven,
           Connecticut
1982   *Aspects of British Art*, British Council tour in Japan
1983   *As of Now : Peter Moores Liverpool Project*, The Walker Art Gallery,
           Liverpool
1984   *The Hard-Won Image*, Tate Gallery, London. *The British Art Show : Old
           Allegiances and New Directions 1979-84*, City of Birmingham Museum
           and Art Gallery and tour (Arts Council of Great Britain touring
           exhibition)
1984-85   *The Proper Study : Contemporary Figurative Paintings from Britain*, British
           Council tour, New Delhi and Bombay
1985   *The British Show*, British Council tour, Art Gallery of New South
           Wales, Sydney. *Rocks and Flesh*, Norwich School of Art Gallery,
           Norwich and tour. *Human Interest : Fifty Years of British Art About People*,
           Cornerhouse, Manchester
1986   *Forty Years of Modern Art 1945-1985*, Tate Gallery, London
1987   *Current Affairs*, Museum of Modern Art, Oxford and British Council
           tour. *British Art in the 20th Century : The Modern Movement*, Royal Academy
           of Arts, London
1987-88   *A School of London : Six Figurative Painters*, British Council tour,
           Kunstnernes Hus, Oslo. *British Figurative Painting : A Matter of Paint*,
           Pamela Auchincloss Gallery, Santa Barbara, California and tour. *Past
           and Present*, Manchester City Art Gallery and tour (Arts Council of
           Great Britain touring exhibition)
1988   *The British Picture*, L.A. Louver, Venice, California

38
Frank Auerbach
Head of E.O.W.
1954

39
Frank Auerbach
E.O.W. on Her Blue Eiderdown
1965

40
Frank Auerbach
Looking Towards Mornington Crescent Station, Night
1972-3

41
Frank Auerbach
Head of J.Y.M.
1974-5

42
Frank Auerbach
Tree on Primrose Hill
1984–5

43
Frank Auerbach
Head of Catherine Lampert II
1988

FRANCIS BACON

1909   Born in Dublin of English parents

Lives and works in London

Selected solo exhibitions

1934	Transition Gallery, London
1949-54,59	Hanover Gallery, London
1953	Beaux Arts Gallery, London
1955	Institute of Contemporary Arts, London
1960,63,65, 67,83,85	Marlborough Fine Art, London
1962	Retrospective exhibition, Tate Gallery, London and tour
1963-64	Solomon R. Guggenheim Museum, New York and tour
1965	Retrospective exhibition, Kunstverein, Hamburg and tour
1967	Marlborough Galleria d'Arte, Rome
1968	Marlborough-Gerson Gallery, New York
1971-72	Retrospective exhibition, Grand Palais, Paris and tour
1975	*Recent Painting 1968-74*, Metropolitan Museum of Art, New York. Marlborough Gallery, Zurich
1977-78	Museo de Arte Moderno, Mexico and tour
1980,84,87	Marlborough Gallery, New York
1985-86	Second retrospective exhibition, Tate Gallery, London and tour
1987	Galerie Lelong, Paris

Selected group exhibitions

1933	*Art Now*, Mayor Gallery, London
1937	*Young British Painters*, Thomas Agnew & Sons, London
1945	*Recent Paintings by Bacon, Hodgkin, Moore, Sutherland and Matthew Smith*, Lefevre Gallery, London
1946	*Recent Paintings by Nicholson, Sutherland, Bacon, Colquhoun, Craxton, Freud, MacBryde and Trevelyan*, Lefevre Gallery, London. *Exposition de Peintures Modernes*, UNESCO, Musée d'Art Moderne, Paris
1948	*Forty Years of Modern Art*, Institute of Contemporary Arts at the Academy Hall, London
1950	*Last Fifty Years of British Art 1900-1950*, Knoedler Galleries, New York
1952	*Present Trends in Realist Painting*, Institute of Contemporary Arts, London
1954	*Venice Biennale*, British Pavilion (with Freud and Nicholson)
1955	*The New Decade*, Museum of Modern Art, New York and tour
1956-57	*Masters of British Painting 1800-1950*, Museum of Modern Art, New York and tour
1958	*Three Masters of British Painting*, Arts Council of Great Britain touring exhibition
1962	*Primitives to Picasso*, Royal Academy of Arts, London
1963	*British Painting in the Sixties*, Tate Gallery, London
1969	*Contemporary Art – Dialogue between East and West*, National Museum of Modern Art, Tokyo
1971	*British Painting and Sculpture 1960-70*, National Gallery of Art, Washington DC
1972-73	*Decade: Painting, Sculpture and Drawing in Britain 1940-49*, Whitechapel Art Gallery, London and tour
1977	*British Painting 1952-1977*, Royal Academy of Arts, London
1978	*Documenta VI*, Kassel
1981	*A New Spirit in Painting*, Royal Academy of Arts, London
1981-82	*Eight Figurative Painters*, Yale Center for British Art, New Haven, Connecticut
1984	*The Hard-Won Image*, Tate Gallery, London
1984-85	*The Proper Study: Contemporary Figurative Paintings from Britain*, British Council tour, New Delhi and Bombay
1985	*Human Interest: Fifty Years of British Art About People*, Cornerhouse, Manchester. *The British Show*, British Council tour, Art Gallery of New South Wales, Sydney
1986	*Forty Years of Modern Art 1945-1985*, Tate Gallery, London
1987	*British Art in the 20th Century: The Modern Movement*, Royal Academy of Arts, London. *Current Affairs*, Museum of Modern Art, Oxford and British Council tour

1987-88	*A School of London: Six Figurative Painters*, British Council tour, Kunstnernes Hus, Oslo
1987	*British Art in the 20th Century: The Modern Movement*, Royal Academy of Arts, London
1988	*The British Picture*, L. A. Louver Gallery, Venice, California. *Exhibition Road: Painters at the Royal College of Art*, Royal College of Art, London

44
Francis Bacon
Figures in a Landscape
1956-7

45 OPPOSITE
Francis Bacon
Portrait of Henrietta Moraes
1965

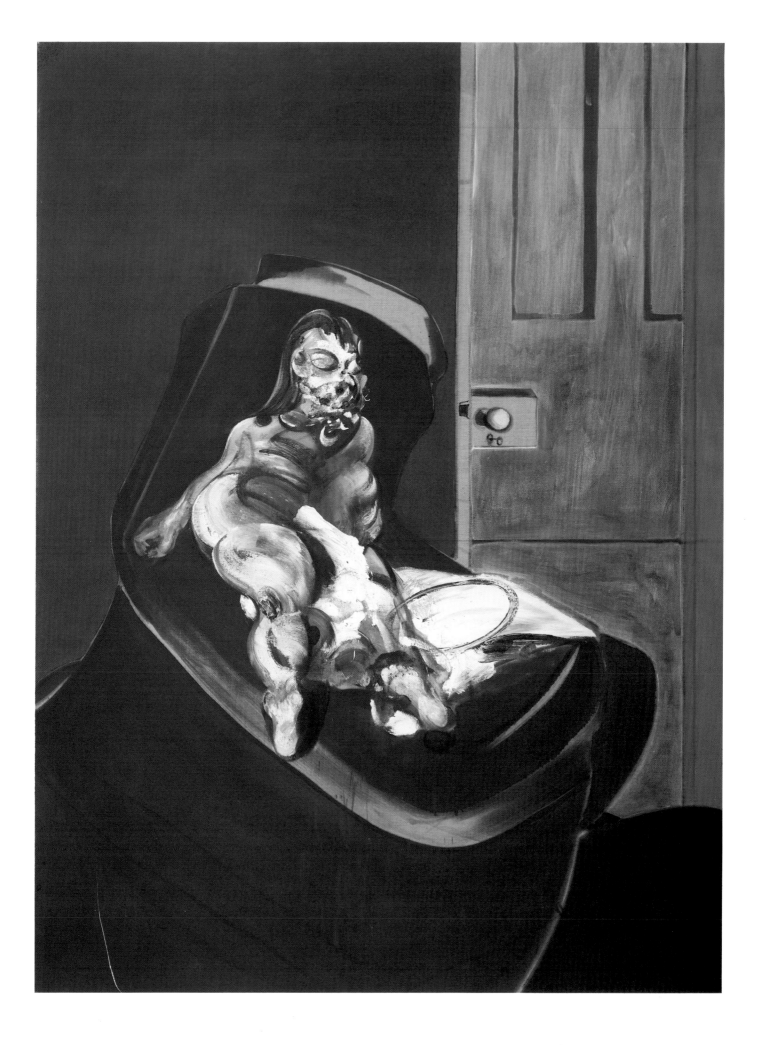

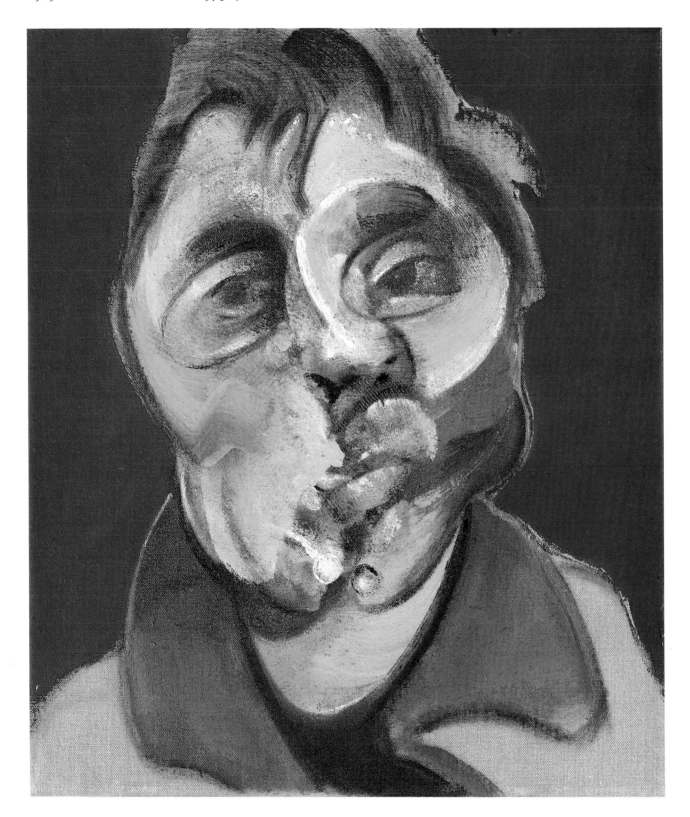

48
Francis Bacon
Portrait of John Edwards
1988

LUCIAN FREUD

1922	Born in Berlin
1933	Moved to Britain
1939	Naturalized as British subject
1938-39	Studied at Central School of Arts and Crafts, London
1939-42	Studied at the East Anglian School of Painting and Drawing, Dedham under Cedric Morris
1942-43	Part-time study at Goldsmiths' College, London
1946-47	Painted in Paris and Greece
1951	Arts Council prize, Festival of Britain
1953-54	Visitor, Slade School of Fine Art, London
1983	Created a Companion of Honour

Lives and works in London

Selected solo exhibitions

1944,46	Lefevre Gallery, London
1947,48	The London Gallery
1950,52	Hanover Gallery, London
1954	*Venice Biennale*, British Pavilion
1958,63,68	Marlborough Fine Art, London
1972,78,82	Anthony d'Offay, London
1974	Retrospective exhibition, Hayward Gallery, London and tour
1979	Nishimura Gallery, Tokyo. Davis & Long Co., New York
1983	Thomas Agnew & Sons, London
1987-88	*Lucian Freud: Paintings*, Hirshorn Museum, Washington DC; Centre Georges Pompidou, Paris; Hayward Gallery, London; Neue Nationalgalerie, Berlin; Scottish National Gallery of Modern Art, Edinburgh
1987-88	*Lucian Freud: works on paper*, Hayward Gallery, London and tour

Selected group exhibitions

1948	*Forty Years of Modern Art*, Institute of Contemporary Arts, London
1950	*London–Paris*, Institute of Contemporary Arts, London
1951	*Sixty Paintings for '51'*, Arts Council of Great Britain, London. *British Painting 1925-50*, Arts Council of Great Britain, London
1952	*Recent Trends in Realist Painting*, Institute of Contemporary Arts, London
1963	*British Painting in the Sixties*, Tate Gallery, London
1966	*British Painting Since 1945*, Tate Gallery, London
1976	*The Human Clay*, Hayward Gallery, London and tour (Arts Council of Great Britain touring exhibition). *Real Life: Peter Moores Liverpool Project 7*, Walker Art Gallery, Liverpool
1977	*British Painting 1952-77*, Royal Academy of Arts, London
1979-80	*The British Art Show*, Mappin Art Gallery, Sheffield and tour (Arts Council of Great Britain touring exhibition)
1981	*A New Spirit in Painting*, Royal Academy of Arts, London
1981-82	*Eight Figurative Artists*, Yale Center for British Art, New Haven, Connecticut
1984	*The Hard-Won Image*, Tate Gallery, London
1984-85	*The Proper Study: Contemporary Figurative Paintings from Britain*, British Council tour, New Delhi and Bombay
1985	*A Singular Vision*, Royal Albert Memorial Museum and Art Gallery, Exeter and tour. *Human Interest: Fifty Years of British Art About People*, Cornerhouse, Manchester
1986	*Forty Years of Modern Art: 1945-1985*, Tate Gallery, London
1987-88	*A School of London: Six Figurative Painters*, British Council tour, Kunstnernes Hus, Oslo
1987	*British Art in the 20th Century: The Modern Movement*, Royal Academy of Arts, London
1988	*The British Picture*, L.A. Louver Gallery, Venice, California

49
Lucian Freud
Girl with Beret
1951

50
Lucian Freud
Large Interior, Paddington
1968-9

51
Lucian Freud
Frank Auerbach
1975-6

52 OPPOSITE
Lucian Freud
Naked Girl with Egg
1980-1

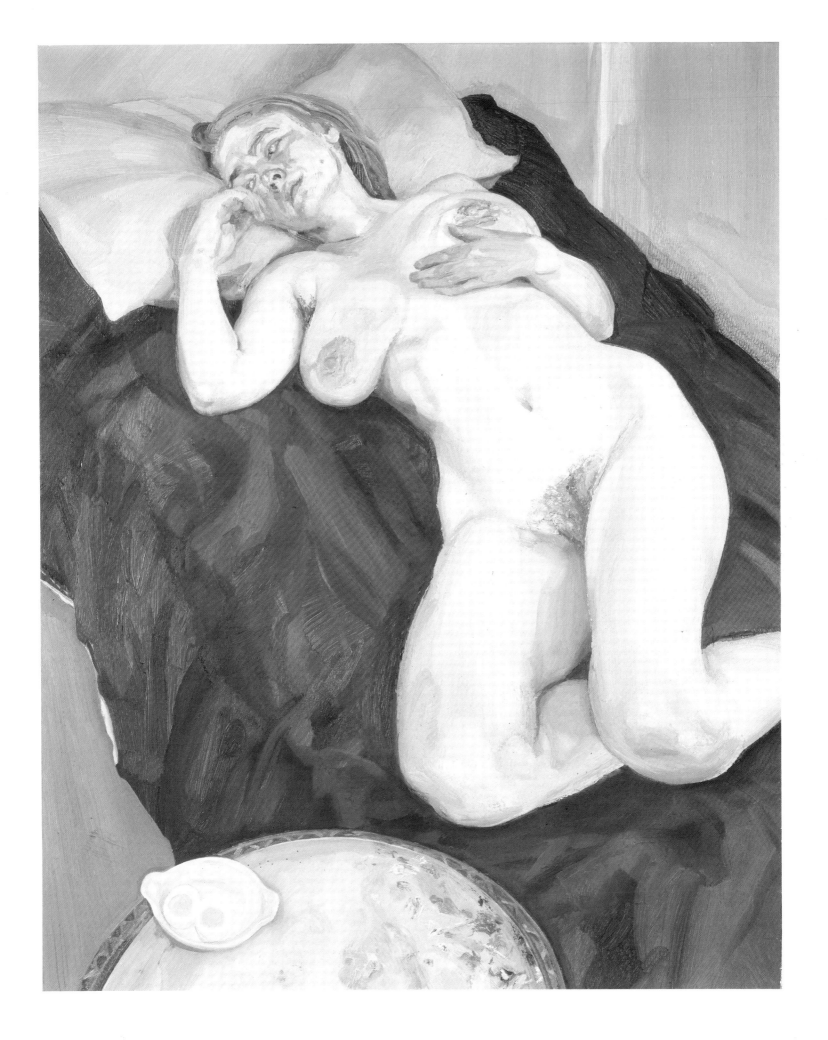

53 OPPOSITE
Lucian Freud
Two Irishmen in W.11
1984-5

54 ABOVE
Lucian Freud
Reflection (Self-Portrait)
1985

LEON KOSSOFF

1926	Born in London
1945-48	Military service in France, Belgium, Holland and Germany
1949-53	Studied at St Martin's School of Art and with David Bomberg at the Borough Polytechnic, London
1953-56	Royal College of Art, London

Lives and works in London

Selected solo exhibitions

1957-64	Six one-man exhibitions at the Beaux Arts Gallery, London
1966	Marlborough Fine Art, London
1972	Whitechapel Art Gallery, London
1973,75,79, 84	Fischer Fine Art, London
1981	*Recent Drawings*, Riverside Studios, London. *Paintings from a Decade 1970-80*, Museum of Modern Art, Oxford
1982,84	L.A.Louver Gallery, Venice, California
1983	Hirschl and Adler Modern, New York
1988	Anthony d'Offay Gallery, London. Robert Miller Gallery, New York

Selected group exhibitions

1964	*54-64 Painting and Sculpture of a Decade*, Tate Gallery, London
1967	*Recent British Painting from the Peter Stuyvesant Foundation Collection*, Tate Gallery, London
1974	*British Painting '74*, Hayward Gallery, London
1976	*The Human Clay*, Hayward Gallery, London and tour (Arts Council of Great Britain touring exhibition)
1977	*British Painting 1952-77*, Royal Academy of Arts, London
1979	*The Hayward Annual*, Hayward Art Gallery, London
1979-80	*The British Art Show*, Mappin Art Gallery, Sheffield and tour (Arts Council of Great Britain touring exhibition)
1981-82	*Eight Figurative Painters*, Yale Center for British Art, New Haven, Connecticut
1984	*The Hard-Won Image*, Tate Gallery, London. *The British Art Show: Old Allegiances and New Directions 1979-84*, City of Birmingham Museum and Art Gallery and tour (Arts Council of Great Britain touring exhibition)
1984-85	*The Proper Study: Contemporary Figurative Paintings from Britain*, British Council tour, New Delhi and Bombay
1985	*The British Show*, British Council tour, Art Gallery of New South Wales, Sydney. *Rocks and Flesh*, Norwich School of Art Gallery, Norwich and tour. *Human Interest: Fifty Years of British Art About People*, Cornerhouse, Manchester
1987	*British Art in the 20th Century: The Modern Movement*, Royal Academy of Arts, London
1987	*Current Affairs*, Museum of Modern Art, Oxford and British Council tour
1987-88	*British Figurative Painting: A Matter of Paint*, Pamela Auchincloss Gallery, Santa Barbara, California and tour. *Past and Present*, Manchester City Art Gallery and tour (Arts Council of Great Britain touring exhibition). *A School of London: Six Figurative Painters*, British Council tour, Kunsternernes Hus, Oslo
1988	*The British Picture*, L.A.Louver, Venice, California. *Exhibition Road: Painters at the Royal College of Art*, Royal College of Art, London

Leon Kossoff
Outside Kilburn Underground, Spring 1976

JOHN LESSORE

1939   Born in London
1957-61   Studied at the Slade School of Fine Art under Thomas Monnington

Lives and works in London and France

Selected solo exhibitions
1965   Beaux Arts Gallery, London
1969   Ashgate Gallery, Farnham
1971   New Art Centre, London
1981   Theo Waddington, London
1983,85   Stoppenbach & Delestre, London
1986   *Working Drawings*, Manor House Society at The Sternberg Centre for Judaism, London
1990   Nigel Greenwood Gallery, London

Selected group exhibitions
1968   *Helen Lessore and the Beaux Arts Gallery*, Marlborough Fine Art, London
1976   *The Human Clay*, Hayward Gallery, London and tour (Arts Council of Great Britain touring exhibition)
1980   *Pictures for an Exhibition*, Whitechapel Art Gallery, London
1981   *Drawings and Watercolours by 13 British Artists*, Marlborough Fine Art, London
1982   *The John Moores Liverpool Exhibition 13*, Walker Art Gallery, Liverpool
1984   *The Hard-Won Image*, Tate Gallery, London
1984-85   *The Proper Study: Contemporary Figurative Paintings from Britain*, British Council tour, New Delhi and Bombay
1985   *Rocks and Flesh*, Norwich School of Art Gallery, Norwich. *A Singular Vision*, Royal Albert Memorial Museum and Art Gallery, Exeter and tour
1986   *Seven British Artists: Figure and Landscape*, Edward Totah Gallery, London
1987-88   *British Figurative Painting: A Matter of Paint*, Pamela Auchincloss Gallery, Santa Barbara, California and tour

61
John Lessore
Paule and Rémi I
1963

62

John Lessore
The Life Room, Norwich School of Art
1980-1

63
John Lessore
La Farine, Villemoustaussou
1981 - 4

64
John Lessore
The Garth
1982 - 3

65
John Lessore
Artist and Model I
1988-9

EUAN UGLOW

1932	Born in London
1948-50	Camberwell School of Arts and Crafts. Awarded David Murray Scholarship
1951-54	Slade School of Fine Art
1952	Spanish State Scholarship to work in Segovia, Spain
1953	Awarded Abbey Minor Travelling Scholarship to France, Holland and Belgium. Also spent six months in Italy
1957	Working in Spain and France. Visited Giacometti with David Sylvester
1959	Moved to studio in Battersea where he still works
1960	Elected member of the London Group
1961-	Part-time teaching at the Slade School of Fine Art and Camberwell School of Arts and Crafts
1972	Won first prize for *Nude, from Twelve Regular Vertical Positions from the Eye 1967* at *The John Moores Liverpool Exhibition 8*, Walker Art Gallery, Liverpool
1972-74	Worked in Italy
1980,85	Worked in Cyprus

Selected solo exhibitions

1961	Beaux Arts Gallery, London
1969	*Drawings*, Gardner Centre, Sussex University, Brighton
1974	Whitechapel Art Gallery, London and tour. *Drawings*, Colnaghi, London
1977,83	Browse and Darby, London
1989	Retrospective exhibition, Whitechapel Art Gallery, London. *Drawings*, Browse and Darby, London

Selected group exhibitions

1960-61	*Modern British Portraits*, The Arts Council Gallery, Cambridge and tour
1961	*The John Moores Liverpool Exhibition 3*, Walker Art Gallery, Liverpool
1962	*Six Young Painters*, Cheltenham Art Gallery and Museum
1964	*London Group 1914-64, Jubilee Exhibition: Fifty Years of British Art*, Tate Gallery, London and tour
1968	*Helen Lessore and the Beaux Arts Gallery*, Marlborough Fine Art, London
1971	*Painting and Perception*, The MacRobert Arts Centre Gallery, University of Stirling. *The Slade 1871-1971*, Royal Academy of Arts, London
1972	*The John Moores Liverpool Exhibition 8*, Walker Art Gallery, Liverpool
1975	*Body and Soul: Peter Moores Liverpool Project 3*, Walker Art Gallery, Liverpool
1976	*The Human Clay*, Hayward Gallery, London and tour (Arts Council of Great Britain touring exhibition)
1977	*British Painting 1952-77*, Royal Academy of Arts, London
1979	*Hayward Annual*, Hayward Gallery, London
1979-80	*The British Art Show*, Mappin Art Gallery, Sheffield and tour (Arts Council of Great Britain touring exhibition)
1981	*Eight Figurative Painters*, Yale Center for British Art, New Haven, Connecticut. *From Object to Object*, Worcester City Museum and Art Gallery and tour (Arts Council of Great Britain touring exhibition)
1984	*The Hard-Won Image*, Tate Gallery, London
1984-85	*The Proper Study: Contemporary Figurative Paintings from Britain*, British Council tour, New Delhi and Bombay
1984-85	*The Singular Vision*, Royal Albert Memorial Museum and Art Gallery, Exeter and tour
1986	*Studies of the Nude*, Marlborough Fine Art, London

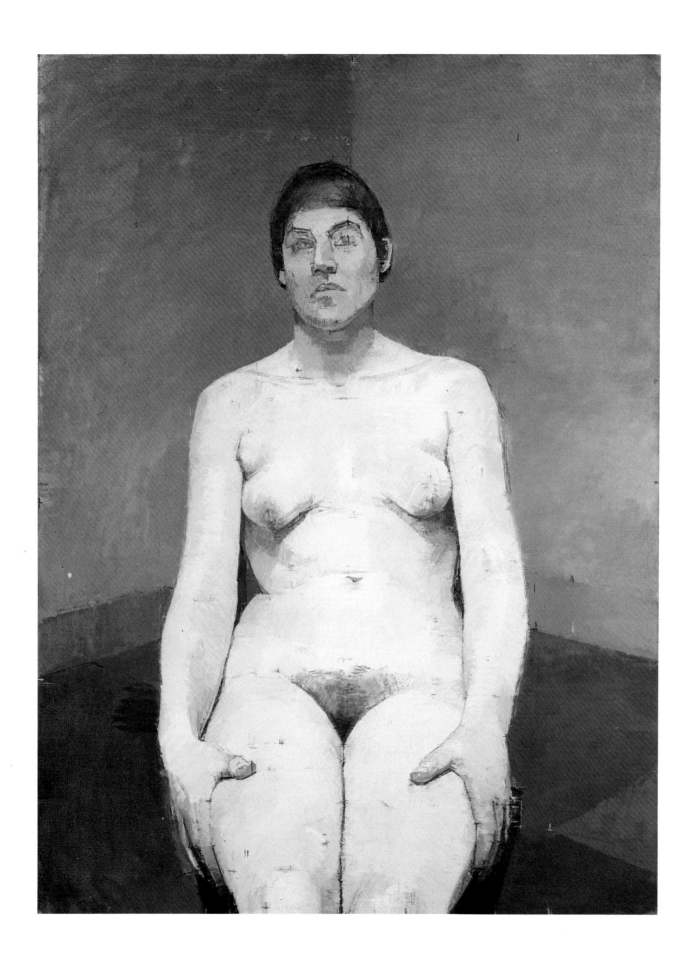

66 OPPOSITE
Euan Uglow
The German Girl
1961-2

67 RIGHT
Euan Uglow
Nude, from Twelve Regular Vertical Positions from the Eye
1967

68
Euan Uglow
Portrait of Eve
1969

69
Euan Uglow
Curled Nude on a Stool
1982-3

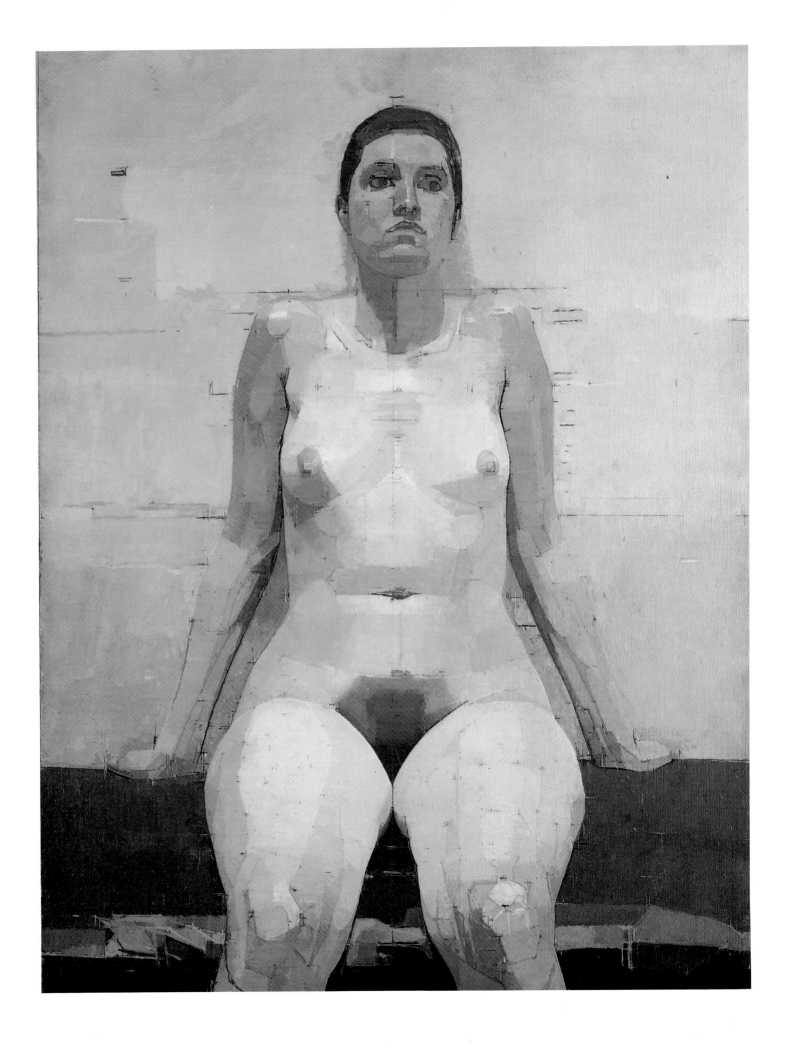

70 OPPOSITE
Euan Uglow
Celebration of the New Skylight
1986 – 7

71 BELOW
Euan Uglow
Fruit Pyramid
1988

JOHN WONNACOTT

1940	Born in London
1958-63	Studied at the Slade School of Fine Art

Lives and works in Leigh-on-Sea, Essex

Selected solo exhibitions

1977	The Minories, Colchester
1978	Rochdale Art Gallery and tour
1980,85,88	Marlborough Fine Art, London
1986	Scottish National Portrait Gallery, Edinburgh

Selected group exhibitions

1971	*Painting and Perception*, The MacRobert Arts Centre Gallery, University of Stirling
1974	*British Painting '74*, Hayward Gallery, London
1977	*British Painting 1952-77*, Royal Academy of Arts, London
1984	*The Hard-Won Image*, Tate Gallery, London
1981	*Drawings and Watercolours by 13 British Artists*, Marlborough Fine Art, London
1983	*Britain Salutes New York*, Marlborough Gallery Inc, New York
1986-87	*Foundation Veranneman invites Marlborough*, Foundation Veranneman, Kruishoutem, Belgium
1988	*Works on Paper by Contemporary Artists*, Marlborough Fine Art, London
1989	*Salute to Turner*, Thomas Agnew & Sons, London

72
John Wonnacott
Grey Self-Portrait
1967 - 74

73
John Wonnacott
Norwich School of Art
1982 - 4

John Wonnacott

Sir Adam Thomson in Hangar 3 with Boeing 747, Night Shift

1985-6

76
John Wonnacott
The Crabbing Bridge
1986-7

Catalogue

The selection of paintings will vary from venue to venue

All measurements are given in centimetres; height before width

Walter Richard Sickert

1 *Mamma Mia Poveretta* c.1903-4
Oil on canvas
46.1 × 38.2
Manchester City Art Galleries

2 *Le Lit de Cuivre* c.1906
Oil on canvas
39.4 × 49.5
Royal Albert Memorial Museum and Art Gallery, Exeter

3 *Hubby and Marie* c.1912
Oil on canvas
51 × 40.7
Manchester City Art Galleries

4 *La Scierie de Torqueville* 1913
Oil on canvas
64.8 × 106.7
Dundee Art Gallery and Museums

5 *Interior with Nude* 1914
Oil on canvas
50.8 × 40.8
Manchester City Art Galleries

6 *Victor Lecour* 1922-4
Oil on canvas
81.3 × 60.5
Manchester City Art Galleries

7 *Portrait of Hugh Walpole* 1929
Oil on canvas
76.2 × 63.5
Glasgow City Museums and Art Galleries

8 *High Steppers* c.1938-9
Oil on canvas
132 × 122.5
Scottish National Gallery of Modern Art, Edinburgh

9 *Alexander Gavin Henderson, 2nd Lord Faringdon*
Oil on canvas
231 × 85
Lord Faringdon

10 *The Temple Bar* c.1941
Oil on canvas
68.5 × 76
Private collection

David Bomberg

11 *Mount Zion with the Church of the Dormition: Moonlight* 1923
Oil on canvas
40.6 × 51
Ben Uri Society, London

12 *Jerusalem, Looking to Mount Scopus* 1925
Oil on canvas
56.2 × 75.5
Trustees of the Tate Gallery

13 *Toledo and River Tajo* 1929
Oil on canvas
58.4 × 76.2
Oldham Art Gallery

14 *Ronda: In the Gorge of the Tajo* 1935
Oil on canvas
92.7 × 72.3
Private collection

15 *Sunrise in the Mountains, Picos de Asturias* 1935
Oil on canvas
59.3 × 67
Private collection

16 *Self-Portrait* 1937
Oil on canvas
75.5 × 55
Scottish National Gallery of Modern Art, Edinburgh

17 *Evening in the City of London* 1944
Oil on canvas
69.8 × 90.8
The Museum of London

18 *Castle Ruins, St Hilarion, Cyprus* 1948
Oil on canvas
95.3 × 127.6
Trustees of the National Museums and Galleries on Merseyside (Walker Art Gallery, Liverpool)

19 *Portrait of Dinora* 1952
Oil on canvas
94.4 × 71.1
Fischer Fine Art Ltd, London

Stanley Spencer

20 *Cottages at Burghclere* c.1930-1
Oil on canvas
62.2 × 160
Syndics of the Fitzwilliam Museum, Cambridge

21 *Self-Portrait with Patricia Preece* 1936
Oil on canvas
61 × 91.2
Syndics of the Fitzwilliam Museum, Cambridge

22 *Hilda, Unity and Dolls* 1937
Oil on canvas
76.2 × 50.8
Leeds City Art Galleries

23 *The Vale of Health, Hampstead* 1939
Oil on canvas
60.9 × 81.3
Glasgow City Museums and Art Galleries

24 *Seated Nude* 1942
Oil on canvas
76.2 × 50.8
Private collection

25 *The Psychiatrist* 1945
Oil on canvas
74.9 × 49.5
Birmingham City Museums and Art Gallery

26 *Portrait of Dame Mary Cartwright, FRS, ScD* 1958
Oil on canvas
76 × 49.5
The Mistress and Fellows of Girton College, Cambridge

William Coldstream

27 *Portrait of Stephen Spender* 1937
Oil on canvas
91.4 × 66
Private collection

28 *Cripplegate* c.1946-7
Oil on canvas
78.7 × 91.4
Arts Council Collection, South Bank Centre, London

29 *Reclining Nude* 1953-4
Oil on canvas
87 × 134.5
Arts Council Collection, South Bank Centre, London

30 *Seated Nude* 1960
Oil on canvas
106.7 × 71.1
Private collection

31 *Standing Nude* 1977-8
Oil on canvas
101 × 61
Mr & Mrs Donald Lenox

32 *Westminster VI* 1978
Oil on canvas
76.2 × 71.1
The Forward Trust Group

Michael Andrews

33 *The Family in the Garden* 1960-2
Oil on canvas
198.2 × 299.8
Calouste Gulbenkian Foundation, Lisbon, Portugal

34 *The Colony Room I* 1962
Oil on hardboard
121.9 × 182.9
Private collection

35 *Lights II: The Ship Engulfed* 1972
Acrylic on canvas
183 × 153.5
Arts Council Collection, South Bank Centre, London

36 *Sax a.d. 832* 1982
Oil and acrylic on canvas
152.4 × 152.4
Private collection courtesy Anthony d'Offay Gallery

37 *Self-Portrait* 1988
Oil on board
25 × 20.3
Private collection courtesy Anthony d'Offay Gallery

Frank Auerbach

38 *Head of E.O.W.* 1954
Oil on canvas
45.8 × 30.5
Private collection

39 *E.O.W. on Her Blue Eiderdown* 1965
Oil on board
59.7 × 81.3
Torquil and Anne Norman

40 *Looking Towards Mornington Crescent Station, Night* 1972-3
Oil on board
127 × 127
Sheffield City Art Galleries

41 *Head of J.Y.M.* 1974-5
Oil on board
61 × 71
Marlborough Fine Art, London

42 *Tree on Primrose Hill* 1984-5
Oil on canvas
122.6 × 148.6
The British Council

43 *Head of Catherine Lampert II* 1988
Oil on canvas
74.9 × 66
Private collection

Francis Bacon

44 *Figures in a Landscape* 1956-7
Oil on canvas
152.5 × 118
Birmingham City Museums and Art Gallery

45 *Portrait of Henrietta Moraes* 1965
Oil on canvas
198 × 147.5
Manchester City Art Galleries

46 *Self-Portrait* 1969
Oil on canvas
35.5 × 30.5
Private collection

47 *Study for a Human Body (Man Turning on the Light)* 1973-4
Oil and acrylic on canvas
198 × 147.5
Royal College of Art, London

48 *Portrait of John Edwards* 1988
Oil on canvas
198 × 147.5
Marlborough Fine Art, London

Lucian Freud

49 *Girl with Beret* 1951
Oil on canvas
35.6 × 25.4
Manchester City Art Galleries

50 *Large Interior, Paddington* 1968-9
Oil on canvas
183 × 122
Thyssen-Bornemisza Collection, Lugano, Switzerland

51 *Frank Auerbach* 1975-6
Oil on canvas
40 × 26.5
Roberts & Hiscox Ltd

52 *Naked Girl with Egg* 1980-1
Oil on canvas
75 × 60.5
The British Council

53 *Two Irishmen in W.11* 1984-5
Oil on canvas
172.7 × 141.6
Private collection

54 *Reflection (Self-Portrait)* 1985
Oil on canvas
56.2 × 51.2
Private collection

55 *Painter and Model* 1986-7
Oil on canvas
159.6 × 120.7
Private collection

Leon Kossoff

56 *Father seated in Armchair* 1960
Oil on board
152.4 × 111.8
Private collection courtesy Anthony d'Offay Gallery

57 *Railway Landscape near King's Cross, Summer* 1967
Oil on board
122 × 152.4
Private collection courtesy Anthony d'Offay Gallery

58 *Outside Kilburn Underground, Spring* 1976
Oil on board
122 × 152.4
Private collection courtesy Anthony d'Offay Gallery

59 *Portrait of Chaim* 1985-6
Oil on board
108 × 78
Private collection courtesy Anthony d'Offay Gallery

60 *Christchurch, Spitalfields, Early Summer* 1987
Oil on board
137 × 127
Private collection courtesy Anthony d'Offay Gallery

John Lessore

61 *Paule and Rémi I* 1963
Oil on board
50.8 × 43.2
Private collection

62 *The Life Room, Norwich School of Art* 1980-1
Oil on board
122 x 183
Private collection

63 *La Farine, Villemoustaussou* 1981-4
Oil on board
76.2 × 152.4
Private collection

64 *The Garth* 1982-3
Oil on board
91.4 × 152.4
Robert Stoppenbach

65 *Artist and Model I* 1988-9
Oil on board
152 × 203
Robert Stoppenbach and Nigel Greenwood

Euan Uglow

66 *The German Girl* 1961-2
Oil on canvas
102.9 × 77.5
Arts Council Collection, South Bank Centre, London

67 *Nude, from Twelve Regular Vertical Positions from the Eye* 1967
Oil on board
244 × 91.5
University of Liverpool Art Collections

68 *Portrait of Eve* 1969
Oil on canvas on board
47.6 diameter
C. von Schmieder

69 *Curled Nude on a Stool* 1982-3
Oil on canvas
77.7 × 100
Ferens Art Gallery, City of Kingston-upon-Hull Museums and Art Galleries

70 *Celebration of the New Skylight* 1986-7
Oil on canvas
90 × 70
Bernard Jacobson Gallery

71 *Fruit Pyramid* 1988
Oil on canvas on board
28 × 27.3
Browse and Darby

John Wonnacott

72 *Grey Self-Portrait* 1967-74
Oil on board
182.9 × 76.2
Private collection, USA

73 *Norwich School of Art* 1982-4
Oil on canvas
198 × 259
Trustees of the Tate Gallery

74 *Portrait of Sir Adam Thomson* 1985-6
Oil on board
243.9 × 243.9
Scottish National Portrait Gallery, Edinburgh

75 *Sir Adam Thomson in Hangar 3 with Boeing 747, Night Shift* 1985-6
Oil on board
243.9 × 243.9
Sir Adam Thomson

76 *The Crabbing Bridge* 1986-7
Oil on canvas
152.4 × 152.4
Private collection

List of Lenders

Photographic acknowledgements